AFRICAN~AMERICAN FAITH *in* AMERICA

LARRY G. MURPHY

J. GORDON MELTON, SERIES EDITOR

Facts On File, Inc.

AFRICAN-AMERICAN FAITH IN AMERICA
Faith in America

Facts On File, Inc.
132 West 31st Street
New York NY 10001

Library of Congress Cataloging-in-Publication Data
Murphy, Larry (Larry G.)
African-American faith in America / Larry Murphy
p. cm. — (Faith in America)
Includes bibliographical references and index.
ISBN-13: 978-0-8160-4990-5
ISBN-10: 0-8160-4990-4
1. African Americans—Religion. I. Title. II. Series

BR563.N4 M87 2002
200'.89'96073—dc21 2002028593

Facts On File books are available at special discounts when purchased in bulk quantities for businesses, associations, institutions, or sales promotions. Please call our Special Sales Department in New York at (212) 967-8800 or (800) 322-8755.

You can find Facts On File on the World Wide Web at http://www.factsonfile.com

Produced by the Shoreline Publishing Group LLC
Editorial Director: James Buckley Jr.
Contributing Editors: Beth Adelman, Martha Southgate
Designed by Thomas Carling, Carling Design, Inc.
Photo research by Laurie Schuh
Index by Nanette Cardon, IRIS

Photo and art credits:
Cover: Corbis (top; bottom left); AP/Wide World (bottom center; bottom right)
AP/Wide World: 41, 45, 57, 58, 60, 65, 74, 82, 86, 96, 104, 114, 117; Chicago Historical Society: 37, 81; Corbis: 6, 15, 18, 27, 32, 84, 106, 110; Courtesy Bethune-Cookman College: 48; Dreamworks/Shooting Star: 89; Wayne Fisher: 24 (Photo taken with the cooperation of the Peabody Room, Georgetown Branch Library of the District of Columbia Public Library); Flower Pentecostal Heritage Center: 42; Hulton-Getty: 21, 53, 67; Library of Congress: 30; Los Angeles Times/J. Emilio Flores: 72.

Dedicated to the late Rev. Dr. Prathia Hall, to the Rev. Dr. Ella Mitchell, and to all "Those Preachin' Women" and praying women who have borne our struggle with courage, strength, and a determined spirit.

Cover printed by Yurchak Printing, Landisville, Pa.
Book printed and bound by Yurchak Printing, Landisville, Pa.
Printed in the United States of America

This book is printed on acid-free paper.

Contents

FOREWORD

AMERICA BEGINS A NEW MILLENNIUM AS ONE OF THE MOST RELIGIOUSLY diverse nations of all time. Nowhere else in the world do so many people—offered a choice free from government influence—identify with such a wide range of religious and spiritual communities. Nowhere else has the human search for meaning been so varied. In America today, there are communities and centers for worship representing all of the world's religions.

The American landscape is dotted with churches, temples, synagogues, and mosques. Zen Buddhist zendos sit next to Pentecostal tabernacles. Hasidic Jews walk the streets with Hindu swamis. Most amazing of all, relatively little conflict has occurred among religions in America. This fact, combined with a high level of tolerance of one another's beliefs and practices, has let America produce people of goodwill ready to try to resolve any tensions that might emerge.

The Faith in America series celebrates America's diverse religious heritage. People of faith and ideals who longed for a better world have created a unique society where freedom of religious expression is a keynote of culture. The freedom that America offers to people of faith means that not only have ancient religions found a home here, but that newer forms of expressing spirituality have also taken root. From huge churches in large cities to small spiritual communities in towns and villages, faith in America has never been stronger. The paths that different religions have taken through American history is just one of the stories readers will find in this series.

Like anything people create, religion is far from perfect. However, its contribution to the culture and its ability to help people are impressive, and these accomplishments will be found in all the books in the series. Meanwhile, awareness and tolerance of the different paths our neighbors take to the spiritual life has become an increasingly important part of citizenship in America.

Today, more than ever, America as a whole puts its faith in freedom—the freedom to believe.

African-American Faith in America

One of the great contributions of the last generation has been to recognize and begin to bring to light the contributions of African Americans in building and shaping American life and culture. Africans began to arrive in North America in the 17th century, brought by force, but bringing their traditional African faiths, as well as Islam, with them. Very soon after settling in, many began to accept the new Christian faith they found in the United States, which they saw through their own unique perspective.

Constituting one of the largest ethnic communities in America, and certainly its most visible, African Americans did not just blindly accept Christianity. As the European Christians before them had done, they remolded the faith to fit their own needs and situations. They then offered the vitality of African-American church life to the larger population in ways that have immensely enriched the contemporary religious world, from spirituals and gospel music to the spread of Pentecostalism and the development of a socially relevant Protestantism. Since the 1930s, African Americans have been doing much the same in the Muslim community, merging its message with new and vibrant methods.

In recent decades, African-American religious leaders have emerged as prominent bishops, imams, church administrators, theologians, and social activists, especially in their work in the Civil Rights movement. Because their people have struggled with the American system, they have discovered new paths for social change that have demonstrated to a wide variety of groups seeking social justice, what can be accomplished. In *African-American Faith in America*, Larry Murphy has pulled together a spectrum of themes to demonstrate the diverse paths by which people of an ancient spirituality have made their way successfully in the contemporary world.

– J. Gordon Melton, Series Editor

INTRODUCTION

The Variety of African-American Faith

WHEN ONE THINKS ABOUT AFRICAN AMERICANS AND RELIGION, often what comes to mind is their involvement in the large families of Methodist and Baptist Christians. While it is true that millions of African Americans are members of those denominations, the descendants of Africa are a people of great variety, and that includes their religious life. One may find them among the members of nearly all of the many religious communities of the United States—Christian, Jewish, Islamic, Buddhist, Humanist, and more. Where did this rich religious diversity come from? When did it start?

American history classes in the United States teach that among the colonial settlers and founders of the nation were persons who came to this land in search of an opportunity to express freely their Christian faith in their daily lives. One of the famous early colonies that we connect with this religious quest was Jamestown, Virginia, settled in 1607. What is less well-known is that just 12 years after Jamestown was settled by people from England, people from Africa arrived there and also became residents, although they were sold to colonists as indentured servants. It appears that among these 20 Africans were persons who were already baptized Christians. And so, African-American Christianity has a long heritage in the United States, going back to its earliest colonial days.

Even less well-known is that Islam was introduced to the United States in colonial days by enslaved Africans. There exist pictures of slaves in Islamic garments and fragments of materials on which slaves wrote by hand from memory sections of the Qur'an, the sacred text of Islam. Some enslaved Africans left evidence of their Muslim faith through other writings or through statements made to interviewers. (For more, see boxes on pages 12 and 24.)

Over the years, African Americans, enslaved and free, joined up with the many branches of Protestant and Catholic Christianity, with Judaism, with Islam, and other religious bodies. But they did so as people who still remembered the religion and culture of the lands from which they had been brought. They did so as people who had a very different place in American society than people who had willingly emigrated here. They did so as people of creative minds and spirits. And so, while the religious life of African Americans came to be similar in many ways to that of other inhabitants of the land, they also developed unique belief systems and ways of professing their faith. This book will explore how this combination of similarity and uniqueness took shape and what African-American religions have received from and contributed to the life of the United States.

PRECEDING PAGE
A terrible beginning
This undated drawing shows a scene from Harriet Beecher Stowe's 1852 novel, Uncle Tom's Cabin, *and illustrates the forced separation of families that was a part of the slave trade in early America.*

Africans in the Americas

When explorers such as Amerigo Vespucci (1454–1512) and Christopher Columbus (1451–1506) made known to Europeans the lands that we now call the Americas, they first thought they would either find vast treasures in gold or seize them from the native inhabitants. Though Spanish adventurers did take home some plundered gold, Spanish and later English colonists soon discovered that the real treasure was in the agricultural produce of the rich soil of these western lands. To make the large plantations that they established productive and profitable, they needed large numbers of farm laborers. The Native Americans who lived on the land were forced to work for the colonists. But the hard labor and harsh treatment of these indigenous people caused them to sicken and die in great numbers. There was danger that they would completely die out.

Spanish Catholic bishop Bartholomeo de Las Casas (1474–1566) tried to protect them from this fate, first by pleading for better treatment, then by suggesting that there was another group of people who

In the Middle Passage
Crammed in the holds of ships, Africans were brought forcibly to America to work as slaves. This contemporary painting imagines what life was like for the unfortunate men, women, and children.

could be used as substitutes for the Indians. Las Casas believed that Africans would make hardier workers and would not suffer the widespread loss of life. They had already shown their strength and endurance as laborers on the plantations that the Portuguese had set up on islands off the coast of North Africa. Accepting his suggestions, Africans began to be purchased as slaves and put to work in all the North and South American islands and mainlands that the Europeans were colonizing.

The Maafa

Writers on the subject of African slavery tell us that some 10 to 12 million persons—male and female, teenage to adult—were shipped from the slave ports of western Africa for sale in the Americas. The process in which this happened was known as the "Triangular Trade." On the first leg of the journey, commercial ships sailed from Europe and England with items for trade, such as guns, alcohol, and fabric; these were exchanged for human cargo on the African coast. The enslaved men, women, and children were then carried to North and South American ports and traded for the commercial produce of those lands. The third and final leg of the journey was back to the starting countries, to sell the cargo and start the process over again.

The second, or middle leg of this three-part voyage, on which Africans were the "cargo," was called the "Middle Passage." The trip could take up to three months, during which time the enslaved would be chained together below decks, packed in tightly to fit the maximum number of persons, thus increasing the potential profit from their sale. Sanitary conditions were very poor. Many became sick and died. They were thrown overboard and the voyage went on. Already feeling the deep pain of being captured and sold away from the places and people they knew and loved, the experience of a long, harsh sea journey into the unknown compounded the misery.

The millions of Africans who were transported to the Americas were made up of persons from many different geographic areas, tribes, languages, and cultural traditions. Their purchasers intentionally separated those from the same place and mixed them with others so that they would not feel kinship to one another nor be able to communicate with one another. Therefore, the chances would be lessened that they would be able to cooperate in any plans for revolt. Thus, the forebears of African Americans were removed from their homelands, separated from people and things familiar to them, and carried to many different destinations, all thousands of miles away from home. This

Remembering the Past

Maafa means "disaster" in the East African language of Kiswahili. It has been adopted by some scholars to describe the scope and tragedy of the North and South American slave trade. These scholars feel that there needs to be special attention paid, using special language, to the holocaust that forced millions of Africans from their homes and brought them here against their will.

St. Paul's Community Baptist Church in Brooklyn, New York, has developed an extraordinary way to remember the Maafa. Every fall, hundreds of members of this large church's congregation plan and execute a week's worth of educational activities, culminating in an extraordinary pageant, lasting about five hours, that re-enacts the entire Middle Passage with music and performance. Hundreds of people attend and are deeply moved and educated about the agony of slavery. The event demonstrates that the African-American church tradition of activism and involvement continues.

series of events has been called the African Diaspora—the "scattering." Millions were taken to the Americas. Millions more—as many as 40 million—died or were left destitute by the processes of capture and transport. Upon arrival in America, they faced the cruelty and abuses of living permanently in slavery, where one was considered to be property and not a person. It is easy to see, then, why some have come to name this experience by the Kiswahili term the *Maafa*—the African Holocaust. One cannot fully understand the forms, the character, or the content of the religions of African Americans if one does not see them as people whose history includes the Maafa.

The Faith of Memory

The people of African societies from which African Americans were descended had rich religious traditions of ancient and deeply held beliefs and practices. These did not vanish from the minds and hearts of the enslaved. Instead, the people remembered significant portions of their religious traditions and carried these with them on the Middle Passage. When they could, the enslaved re-established those traditions in their new American homes. In the Caribbean and Latin America today, it is common to see religious practices that are very much like those one would have seen in African countries centuries ago.

The slavery system in the United States did not allow African practices to continue openly. Part of the reason for this was the fear that re-establishing the African heritage would become a source for renewed African identity and thus solidarity, leading to resistance against slavery. Another part of the reason was the slaveholders' rejection of African culture, which stemmed from their view that it was heathen (not believing in a Christian God) and thus not to be allowed. But secretly, many African religious beliefs and practices were continued, often blending with the religion that the Africans were taught here.

Traditional religion generally refers to religious thoughts and practices that originated in Africa before contact with Christianity or Islam. Although there is great variety in worship and belief, there are some common features in traditional religion. One is the belief that one supreme God created the earth and all that is in it. That God, whom some African peoples picture as male and some as female, cares about the well-being of all things and expects that humans will treat each

Islam

Islam is a religion of submission to Allah (God) and his prophet Muhammad. Muhammad (570–632) founded the faith in the late seventh century, preaching that Allah had revealed to him the laws of Allah, to be followed by all believers. Those laws are now collected in a book—the Qur'an—that many Muslim children memorize in its entirety. (Editor's note: The Muslim scripture book is referred to as either the Koran or as the Qur'an. Though both titles are still in use, the term Qur'an has become more dominant and will be the one used in this book.) Written in Arabic, even Muslims who do not speak that language will sometimes memorize the Qur'an in Arabic. The vast majority of Muslims believe the Qur'an is the final and perfect word of God.

Worldwide, Islam is the world's second-largest religion after Christianity, with more than 1 billion believers worldwide. Though surveys showing the numbers of Muslims in the United States vary, all agree that it is one of the fastest-growing religions in the nation.

Islam came to America in the colonial years, brought by slaves from Africa. In the 20th century, the practice moved from a tiny part of the national religious scene to a slightly larger one with the birth of the Nation of Islam (see page 39).

Today, about 30 percent of America's Muslim population is African-American. Scholars do not agree on the total numbers of Muslims in America; some estimates are about 2 million. As many as 25 percent of America's mosques (Islamic temples) are African-American. The largest national organization of African-American Muslims is the American Muslim Mission, created in the 1970s by Imam Warith Deen Muhammad (b. 1933), son of an early Nation of Islam leader, Elijah Muhammad 1887–1975).

other with fairness, kindness, and respect. Because God cares about all things in creation, humans must also treat the animal and physical world with respect, neither killing animals unnecessarily nor destroying the environment.

The supreme God governs the world through lower spiritual beings who are in charge of specific things, such as rainmaking, the fertility of the soil, the production of iron, and so on. Also, the spirits of certain people important to the community, such as the heads of households, village leaders, and royalty, continue to guide and support the community after those persons have died physically. These are the ancestors. They are not worshiped, as some have mistakenly thought. Rather they are held in high esteem and treated with great respect.

For traditional Africans, living a good life and contributing to the good of the community were important. God expected it, and if you did so, the community would remember you and celebrate you long after you had died. This was the basic meaning of life after death. Not all people did good, however, and some persons were particularly powerful in doing harm (for example, witches). Working against these harmful forces were persons who harnessed the forces of the universe to ward off evil and to defend one from witchcraft ("witch doctors").

New Lands, New Gods

In the Americas, Africans were introduced to European religion. In the United States, that religion was mainly various forms of Protestant Christianity, although in the few places in the British colonies where Catholics settled, Africans were evangelized into that faith as well.

Preachers and teachers from many different denominations worked among the slave population, including Anglicans (later called Episcopalians), the Society of Friends (Quakers), Congregationalists, Presbyterians, Catholics, Methodists, and Baptists. The ones who were most successful were the last two. As African Americans were brought into the Christian faith through these different churches, their beliefs and religious practices were shaped by the doctrines and practices of the faith they joined.

Which Church?

The great majority of black Christians have been nurtured in the Baptist and Methodist denominational families, along with, in the last century, the Church of God in Christ. Today, there are at least four historically black Baptist denominations. In addition, African Americans hold membership in predominantly white Baptist denominations, such as the American Baptist Convention and the Southern Baptist Convention.

Black Baptists believe in full-immersion baptism, as do all Baptists. They are organized congregationally, that is, each local church stands under its own final authority and voluntarily associates with other Baptist congregations in state and national organizations called conventions. They bind themselves to no creed or mandatory statement of faith, but rather are guided by a standard Baptist covenant—a set of statements that represent generally the Baptist understanding of Christian faith and practice.

The three major historically black Methodist denominations operate according to books they call their Discipline, which contain the creeds, the articles of faith, and the denominations' laws and rules of governance. They are very similar in form and content to the

Discipline by which their historical parent body, the United Methodist Church, operates. The Discipline sets forth the structure of the denomination, in which local congregations are administered by pastors who are supervised by bishops through regional officers called presiding elders. The Discipline includes the Apostles Creed, the 25 Articles of Religion, and the order of church liturgies, including Baptism and the Eucharist. Black Methodists, as do Methodists generally, allow for full- immersion baptism, but more typically they will sprinkle or pour the baptismal waters over the candidate's head. Like black Baptists, they celebrate the Eucharist on the first Sunday of each month. Most Baptists will use a simple ceremony of a prayer of consecration over each of the elements (bread and grape juice), whereas Methodists will follow a much more elaborate prescribed liturgy and prayers, such as for confession, adoration, and consecration.

EUCHARIST

This is a ceremony at Christian churches conducted in different ways by different denominations. It recreates the Last Supper, at which Jesus shared bread and wine with his apostles for the last time. Christians recreate this event to remember the promises Jesus made. For their part, Methodists explain sacraments such as this as "an outward and visible sign of an inward and spiritual grace."

Blacks in other traditions, such as Islam and Judaism, tend also to adhere to beliefs and practices that are generally within the scope of what those traditions maintain. However, one strain of African-American Islam, as practiced initially by the Nation of Islam, veered from traditional Islam to incorporate elements of black nationalism, black pride, and some anti-white sentiments. This issue will be explored more in future chapters.

What Makes It a Black Church?

Within the faiths and practices shared with their larger denominational families, African Americans have typically developed beliefs and practices that reflect their own cultural background and historical life experience. The racial abuse and social and legal discrimination which have been persistent since the earliest days in America, regardless of a black individual's economic standing and personal accomplishment, have combined with the fact of a common ethnic and cultural heritage to contribute to some definite similarities in black religious life, in the midst of its diversity.

For instance, whatever the denomination or religious family, worship in African-American congregations will tend to be more intense, lively, and expressive than in their white counterparts, even though there is certainly a range, from the quiet and contemplative to the outright ecstatic. While there may be prescribed orders of service, black congregations will exercise flexibility, allowing for spontaneity

Spread the word
This spire of Bethel Baptist Church rises above Atlanta, Georgia, one of thousands of Christian churches in the United States whose members are predominantly African American, spreading the faith they profess, while addressing that faith to African-American life.

and freedom in the flow of the religious experience. And there is usually an underlying tone of relaxed camaraderie, a sense of family relationship. One result of all this is a usually longer worship service, typically lasting two or more hours.

In the service, music will play a very important role, with some form of congregational, or choral, or instrumental music being present during a substantial part of the worship time. Like Protestantism generally, black worship leans heavily toward the Bible, with the importance of that sacred book being highlighted and also made central to worship through preaching, considered the high point of the service. There are few, if any, greater sources of esteem in black religious communities than the ability to preach with conviction, power, and artistic, creative command of words and ideas—particularly the words and ideas of scripture.

Further, while black religious groups may affirm all the doctrines and creeds of their parent traditions, the parts that are emphasized and how they are interpreted reflect the historical experience of

Black Women: A Special Case

Another important branch of theology that has come from African Americans is Womanist Theology. Womanist Theology points out that while Black Theology applies the faith to the situation of black people, it does not sufficiently recognize that black women have issues and concerns apart from those they share with black men. In fact, black men can and do participate in gender oppression.

Feminist Theology, another late 20th century development, might logically seem to be the umbrella for black women's concerns. But coming as it does largely through white voices, it does not always show sufficient sensitivity to crucial matters of race, nor, in some cases, even embrace black women in full sisterhood.

And so, Womanist Theology voices an understanding of Christian faith that addresses black women's identities of race and gender. It further adds the insight that class is a third critical identity that must be incorporated if one is to have an adequate understanding of the workings of society.

African Americans and who they understand God to be. An important system of belief that results from this has been called Black Theology. Black Theology says that God is the creator and ruler of all things; God declares the dignity and worth of all persons and grants to all the right to a full, free life; God cares about all people, especially the poor and oppressed, and will act to bring about freedom and justice for them.

The Mission of the Black Christian Churches

In the black churches, one can easily see the evidence of both their Christian roots and the concerns that Black and Womanist Theologies address. The most obvious mission of the black churches is evangelism, that is, spreading the faith to more people who are not already members. The centerpiece of black worship services is the sermon. And when the minister delivers her or his message, it typically ends in an appeal for persons to commit themselves to Christ and to join the church. This liturgical element of "opening the doors of the church" or "invitation to Christian discipleship" is so common across congregational, denominational, and regional lines that it clearly marks evangelism as a central mission of black churches.

A second mission is to lead members in a celebration of praise and gratitude to God for God's wondrous, saving works in individual lives and in communal history. Sermons, prayers, songs, and testimonies herald God's love, and God's power to do great things and to deliver people from bad situations. Here are some lines from familiar Christian gospel songs (see more on gospel music in chapter 3):

> *God can do anything but fail.*
> *You don't know what God has done for me; God gave me the victory.*
> *God looked beyond my faults and saw my needs.*
> *Oh, how I love Jesus, because he first loved me.*

The Jesus of black faith is a savior who can guard one's spirit from the destructive forces of life and impart human wholeness in spite of difficult circumstances.

But the black churches generally believe that while God cares about the present and future state of one's soul, God also is concerned in an active way with one's body and one's social condition. And so, the third mission of the black churches is human liberation, particularly focused on black people but extending to all who are oppressed. As an example, here is an excerpt from the Mission Statement of the African Methodist Episcopal (AME) Church, one of the largest black Christian denominations:

> *The mission of the African Methodist Episcopal Church is to minister to the spiritual, intellectual, physical, and emotional needs of all people by spreading Christ's liberating gospel through word and deed.*

This sense of mission across the variety of black denominations has been demonstrated, for instance, through the schools and colleges they have founded, many of them begun in church buildings; the community services they have provided; and the social and political leadership clergy and dedicated laypersons have offered.

African-American faith is a vibrant, living thing—as diverse as the land in which it is followed, but rooted deeply in the land its followers came from.

1

Early Days in America

AFRICANS FIRST CAME TO THE AMERICAS IN THE 15TH CENTURY ON the voyages of Christopher Columbus, and then were part of the Spanish exploratory expeditions. They served as guides, soldiers, and general laborers. In North America, they helped establish settlements across the South and Southwest, from Florida to California. In the early 16th century they also settled in the area that a century later would become Jamestown, Virginia. These Africans intermarried with the Spanish and local Indian peoples, often becoming members of Indian tribes.

But African settlers in the British colonies, in what became the United States, first entered the scene in 1619, when a Dutch military vessel sailed into the port at Jamestown, Virginia, offering to trade its cargo of "twenty negars [Negroes]" for provisions for the ship.

Some of these first 20 Africans to enter the colonies had European names. This indicates that they had already received Christian baptism, since it was the practice then to give all baptized persons a "Christian name," marking their movement from their pre-Christian or "heathen" status into the family of God. Records show that at least two of this group were joined in marriage in a Christian church ceremony. Perhaps those of the 20 Africans who were not Christian became objects of evangelism, as would many who came after them.

SLAVE LESSONS

Here is an excerpt from a catechism (a church instruction manual of beliefs) used for teaching slaves. It demonstrates the way Christian churches taught slaves that God supported slavery:

Question. *Who gave you a master and a mistress?*

Answer.. *God gave them to me.*

Question. *Who says that you must obey them?*

Answer. *God says that I must.*

Question. *What book tells you these things?*

Answer. *The Bible.*

PRECEDING PAGE

A place of their own

By the time of this 1870 drawing, African Americans had fought long and hard for the right to live, work, and worship as they pleased. It was a fight that would continue for decades.

Though it was against accepted practice for Christians to have Christian slaves, by the mid-1600s, church leaders and government lawmakers removed that barrier. A person could "own" a Christian slave, they said, making it legal and acceptable to the church for an African to be both a Christian and a slave. Sermons and materials for religious instruction were composed specifically for use in slave evangelism.

Converting the Enslaved

Many individual clergy and laypersons, including some slaveowners, took up the effort to convert the growing colonial slave population. They saw it as their duty to bring these people they believed to be heathens out of spiritual darkness into the light of Christian faith, to rescue their souls from the horrific eternal damnation that they understood to await all non-believers.

In 1701, the Church of England (Anglicans) organized the Society for the Propagation of the Gospel, which had as one of its main goals the conversion of the African slave population. They chose clergy for this purpose, raised substantial funds, and set up missions at several points along the colonial East Coast. The Society of Friends (Quakers) was active in slave evangelism. Their founder, George Fox, vocally opposed slavery and encouraged Quaker meetings to make the enslaved a part of their religious outreach. Because Catholic presence in early American history was limited primarily to Maryland and Louisiana, Catholic work among African Americans was also limited. But it was not without some success. For instance, in 1785 in Maryland, 3,000 of the state's 15, 000 Catholics were black.

Particularly active and effective among African Americans were preachers of the Methodist and Baptist Churches. These two churches let their clergy move around the country instead of staying tied to church facilities. This let preachers take their message to the people as they moved westward across the landscape. The clergy of both groups tended to be from among the non-elite social ranks and therefore able to relate well to common people. And for the enslaved, it was particularly appealing that Methodist and Baptist leaders spoke out against slavery and encouraged their clergy to have nothing to do with it.

Some persons objected to religious instruction for African slaves. Among the arguments they put forth in their objections were

A pioneering poet
Phillis Wheatley (c.1753–1784) became one of the first African Americans to achieve any sort of artistic fame as a popular poet and writer. Thirty-nine of her poems were published in 1773 as Poems on Various Subjects, Religious and Moral, *her only work. This illustration comes from a later edition of that book.*

these: Would slaves who truly experienced "freedom in Christ" end up resenting and resisting human bondage? Would it make sense for masters and mistresses who became "brothers and sisters in Christ" with African slaves to still hold them in bondage? Therefore would not successful preaching mean having to give up slavery and thus lose one's property? And further, would not the time the enslaved were given for religious instruction mean loss of productive labor time and thus reduced profits for owners? And in any case, would a good English or European Christian want to be "brother or sister" to an African slave?

To deal with some of these issues, the usual Christian teachings were modified so that they conveyed the idea that God supported the slavery system and that it was, therefore, the slave's duty to be obedient and submissive. Some slaveowners, though, never got over their fears and their personal distaste for the slave as Christian, so they prevented their slaves from hearing about Christianity.

There were never enough preachers and religious teachers to serve all of the growing population of Americans, whether black or white, as the country expanded westward in the beginning of the 19th century. There were many Africans, slaves and free, who were not presented with the Christian message. Of those who were, the response was mixed. Some rejected it altogether, being suspicious or resentful of any instruction on holy behavior coming from the class of persons who held them in brutal, enforced bondage. Others continued to hold onto the African religious heritage they remembered.

Of course, many evangelized Africans became believers in Christianity. For them, one attractive feature of Christianity was its teaching about a God who cared for all persons, regardless of their earthly social status; a God whose record in the Bible showed an active commitment to justice and freedom for the oppressed; a God who gave empowerment to the weak and comfort to the abused; a God in whom all persons could take hope for a better life, now and beyond the grave.

Famous Converts

The stories of many of the early African-American converts to Christianity have survived. Phillis Wheatley (c.1753–1784) was purchased as a house servant by the Wheatley family of Boston, around 1761. She quickly gained command of the English language and showed considerable intellectual gifts. She, in fact, became quite knowledgeable about

Remembering Africa

Scholars have debated how much of the African past survived in the United States. Increasing evidence shows that a great deal survived, including religious concepts and worship practices. For instance, some African Americans marked graves with broken bottles and dishes and other small household items in the same manner as one would find at grave sites in Africa. When slaves and former slaves were interviewed by journalists and researchers, they often spoke on subjects in ways that clearly showed the influence of traditional African religious ideas. For instance, former slave Henry F. Pyles told of Old Bab, the "conjure man," who would make "hoodoo hands," or good luck charms, for the young boys and girls. This excerpt is taken from a 1945 book edited by B.A. Botkin and called *Lay My Burden Down: A Folk History of Slavery*:

> *Old Bab Russ live about two miles from me, and I went to him one night at midnight and asked him to make me the hand. I was a young strapper about 16 years old, and thinking about [girls] pretty hard and wanting something to help me out with the one I liked best.*

Pyles said that Old Bab "could talk African or some other unknown tongue, and all the young boys and girls was mortal 'fraid of him." African-American Christians also did the "ring shout," singing and dancing in a circle, which can be traced to West Af-

Western classical poetry and herself wrote and published poetry—the first African American to do so. She was accepted into membership in the Old South (Congregational) Church in Boston. Christian faith was one of the central themes of her poetry.

Henry Evans (1740–1810), freeborn in Virginia, took up ministry to blacks in Fayetteville, North Carolina. Whites viewed such work among blacks as a dangerous disturbance, so Evans had to operate secretly to avoid any hostile reaction from the white citizens. Eventually, whites came to see what they considered an improvement in blacks' behavior, which they associated with Evans' evangelism, so he was given the freedom to preach publicly. He gathered a large following of blacks and whites into a Methodist congregation and built a reputation as an outstanding preacher.

John Marrant and John Stewart share the role of pioneer preachers to Native Americans. Marrant (1755–1791) was converted by the renowned revival preacher George Whitefield (1715–1779). Taken in by the Cherokee tribe in Georgia in his teen years, Marrant converted the chief and the chief's daughter. His efforts with other tribal members met with little success, however. After two years, he returned to his native South Carolina. Later, Marrant spent his time preaching in Nova Scotia, Canada.

John Stewart (1786–1823) established more lasting missionary work among the Wyandot Indians of Upper Sandusky, Ohio. Stewart went through a troubled period in life, was converted in a camp meeting (a worship service often held in large fields and set up much like a camp) in 1814, and devoted the remainder of his years to ministry to the Wyandot. His work led the Methodist Ohio Annual Conference to establish the first official mission to the Indians—in fact the first official Methodist mission to any group. And so, Stewart is credited as the "Father of Missions of the Methodist Episcopal Church."

Lemuel Haynes (1753–1833) achieved the distinction of being the first African American to be ordained in the Congregational Church. He was the pastor of white congregations in Connecticut and Vermont and also became a widely read author.

Church Among the Enslaved

The enslaved had little option as to when and where they worshiped, since their activities were so closely monitored and restricted by the

Islam Among Early African Americans

Not much is known about the earliest followers of Islam in the United States, all of whom were Africans. Among the few names known are Job ben Solomon (1700?–1773?), who was among the first slaves to be freed and return to Africa, and Abdul Rahahman (1762?–1829). They and others first practiced their faith in Africa and brought it with them when they were enslaved and carried to America. There they practiced in traditional ways, when they were allowed, such as praying five times a day and studying the Qur'an.

One well-known early Muslim was a man named Yarrow Mamout (shown in this 1820 painting by James Alexander Simpson). He was brought to this country about 1720 and spent years as a slave in Maryland. He was freed in 1796. Some historians think he was more than 100 years old when he was rescued from the life of a slave. Mamout was known as a faithful Muslim because he refused to eat pork or drink alcohol, forbidden by Islamic law.

Another Muslim was Omar Ibn Said (1770–1864), a religious scholar and trader. Captured in his native Senegal, he was sold into slavery in the Carolinas. His hand-written copy of the Qur'an still survives.

slave system and its supporting civil laws. Owners and authorities did not allow slaves to gather in groups of more than two or three without the presence and supervision of a "trusted" white person, lest the group stray into unacceptable conversations about the fairness of their condition and how they might act together to change it.

But the harshness and hope-challenging nature of their condition was the very reason that they needed to share with one another as a group and seek some form of redeeming hope. And so, slave Christians gathered in secret meetings for worship and religious nurture. They met under cover of night in lonely forest areas, or down by a riverside, or in their cabins. Inventive ways were devised for concealing their activities and suppressing their sounds so they would not be discovered, because that would result in severe punishment. Former slaves tell of making walls for the meeting place out of wet blankets; of gathering in a circle and speaking low to the ground so that the sound would not carry; of speaking and singing into a pail of water, again to capture the sound and prevent any but those immediately around from hearing.

Some slaves were recognized for their outstanding spiritual gifts and persistence in trying to continue their worship, in what the late African-American scholar E. Franklin Frazier called "the invisible institution." Generally forbidden by law to be taught to read and write, many slaves memorized the scriptures they heard in daytime services, including long passages of text. Slave narratives speak of how memorized text was used in these secret meetings, as in this remembrance quoted in Mechal Sobel's 1979 book *Trabelin' On: Slaves' Journey to Afro-Baptist Faith*:

> *De preacher I like the best was Matthew Ewing . . . he sure could read out of his hand. He never learned no real readin' and writin' but he sure knowed his bible and would hold his hand out and make like he was readin' and preach the purtiest preachin' you ever heard.*

Prayer in slave religious meetings was broad in its aims. There were prayers of thanksgiving and praise. The burdens and cares of life were laid before God with requests for the strength to endure. The believer prayed for the power to overcome temptation and persevere in living rightly. And there were prayers for freedom such as, "Lord, deliver us from under bondage."

Invisible Music

The music in the "invisible institution" worship meetings often included hymns learned from whites. But it appears that the songs African-American Christians themselves created were heard even more often in these meetings. The Negro spiritual is perhaps the most original American contribution to world music. Many of the spirituals were built on the African "call and response" format: a lead line, usually done solo, alternating with a repeating choral line. They might show some traces of African thought, as in this reference to the devil's magical powers:

> *De devil is a liar and a conjurer, too;*
> *If you don't look out, he'll conjure you.*

But generally, the spirituals conveyed the slaves' simple Biblical faith. They retold the Biblical narratives, at times as though observing them first-hand. For instance,

> *See dat band all dressed in white?*
> *God's a-going to trouble the water*
> *De leader looks like the Israelite.*
> *God's a-going to trouble the water.*

The spirituals grew out of the slaves' day-to-day life, and so they expressed the full range of their emotions, from piercing sadness and loneliness to calm thoughtfulness; from bursting joy to revolutionary hope.

Another important part of slave religious meetings was preaching. If a slave could back up his or her claim to divine calling with some knowledge of the Bible, evidence of piety, and moving oratorical skills, he or she could emerge as a respected spiritual leader. For the most part, slave "clergy" operated unofficially, without church license. If their owners had confidence that they would deliver sermons that would not challenge slavery or proper slave behavior, they might be permitted to lead worship at approved times. Otherwise, they functioned without the knowledge of their owners.

The religious meeting was deeply meaningful and important to the Christian slave. It was an oasis in what could be an otherwise barren, burdensome journey through life. The significance of the meeting can be seen in these words of a former slave describing slave worshipers (quoted in Louis Hughes' 1969 book, *Thirty Years a Slave*):

> *Their faces seemed to shine with a happy light—their very countenances showed that their souls had been refreshed and that it had been good for them to be there. These meetings were the joy and comfort of the slaves, and even those who did not profess Christianity were calm and thoughtful while in attendance.*

The Walkout

St. George Methodist Church in Philadelphia was the scene of the event that in many ways symbolizes the rise of independent African-American denominations.

African Americans had been part of Methodism from its start in the American colonies. Methodism's founder, John Wesley (1703–1791), personally baptized black converts and was an outspoken critic of slavery. Anne Sweitzer (dates unknown), a black woman, was among the original group of worshipers in the first Methodist church building in the colonies, erected in Maryland by Robert Strawbridge in 1764. A black woman known to history only as Betty was present in 1766 when another Methodist pioneer, Phillip Embry (1728–1775), conducted the first Methodist worship service for those who would become the congregation of the historic John Street Methodist Church, in New York City. Black slaves helped erect the first building to house the John Street Church. When American Methodism was born at a gathering called the "Christmas Conference" of 1784, Harry

Hosier (1750–1806) and Richard Allen (1760-1831), were (non-voting) participants.

Allen was born into slavery in Philadelphia and later he and his parents were sold to a farm in Delaware. Permitted by their owner to receive religious instruction, Allen and his brother were converted by a traveling Methodist preacher. The owner was subsequently converted and allowed Allen and his brother to hire themselves out to earn money with which to purchase their freedom at a much-reduced cost. Sometime around the end of the Revolutionary War in 1781, Allen had purchased his freedom and spent the next several years as a traveling laborer and preacher.

Arriving in Philadelphia in 1786, he and a friend, Absalom Jones (1746–1818), attempted to organize a ministry to black citizens but ran into resistance from both whites and blacks. They did, however, organize the Free African Society, a mutual aid and anti-slavery society that was among the first community organizations. But this pioneer-

Little-known early leader *Rev. Richard Allen was one of the most important religious leaders in the first years of the United States. He helped form one of the first and largest African-American churches, as well as a mutual aid and anti-slavery society.*

ing initiative was just a preview of an even more long-lasting development soon to follow, quite apart from anything Allen and Jones had intended.

Allen, as a Methodist preacher of some reputation, had occasionally been granted the opportunity to preach at St. George, Philadelphia's premier Methodist church. This seems to have attracted an increasing number of blacks to that church. Arriving for Sunday morning service in November of 1787, the black worshipers were informed that they were to take seats in the balcony. Given the attitudes and practices of the times, such segregation probably came as no surprise; the blacks went upstairs as directed. But as they knelt for prayer, the sexton came over to inform them that they were still in the wrong seats, and that their designated place was to the rear of the balcony. When their pleas for a courtesy delay until the prayer ended were curtly met with the threat of physical removal, Allen, Jones, and several others rose and walked out of the sanctuary for good.

THE WALKOUT

Richard Allen wrote about "The Walkout" and its impact in his book *Life Experience and Gospel Labors*:

By the time prayer was over, and we all went out of the church in a body, and they were no more plagued with us in the church. This raised a great excitement and inquiry among the citizens, in so much that I believe they were ashamed of their conduct. But my dear Lord was with us, and we were filled with fresh vigor to get a house erected to worship God in.

The Free African Society served as the venue for worship until a decision was made in 1794 about a permanent worship arrangement. The majority voted to organize as an Episcopal congregation. Though Jones had sided with Allen in favor of forming a Methodist congregation, he consented to lead the majority group and went on to ordination as the priest of St. Thomas Episcopal Church, the first African American to be ordained in the denomination.

Allen chose to remain a Methodist, as he wrote in his book *Life Experience and Gospel Labors of Rt. Rev. Richard Allen*:

> *I was confident that there was no religious sect or denomination which would suit the capacity of the colored people as well as the Methodist; for this plain and simple gospel suits best for any people; for the unlearned can understand, and the learned are sure to understand.*

Allen purchased an old blacksmith's shop and fitted it up as a worship chapel, naming it Bethel African Methodist Church. It is considered the Mother Church of what is today the African Methodist Episcopal (AME) denomination. An anvil, from the blacksmithing setting of the original chapel, remains today in the logo of the denomination.

The Independence Model

What Allen and Jones did in founding St. Thomas and Bethel was part of the developing model for African American organized religious life. They were not the first to set up separate houses of worship. Black Baptists had formed a separate congregation in 1773 at Silver Bluff, South Carolina. Black members of the Methodist congregation in Baltimore had, in 1776, been granted permission to meet for additional worship and devotions apart from the regular integrated service. In 1796, the black members of the John Street Methodist Church in New York City, led by James Varick (1750–1826), were granted a similar request. That group was chartered as a congregation, Zion Church, in 1801. And in 1805, Peter Spencer (1779–1843) led the black members of Asbury Methodist Church in Wilmington, Delaware, to form Ezion Methodist Church. Spencer's group incorporated in 1813 as the Union Church of Africans. Allen's Bethel joined with other separated Methodist congregations in 1816 to incorporate as the African Methodist Episcopal Church. And Varick's congregation joined with others in the region to incorporate in 1821 as what came to be called the African Methodist Episcopal Zion Church.

These moves for independence had a double motivation. On the one hand, African Americans wanted to escape the discriminatory treatment that they typically received in worship settings with whites, such as segregated seating, delay in being served the Eucharist until after whites had been served, and exclusion from full membership privileges. Similar practices were to be expected in the larger world but were especially bitter to experience in what was supposedly the house of God.

African Americans also felt more comfortable with one another, because they shared a common cultural identity and had common experiences in the community because of their color. Worship could be expressed in the styles and forms of their culture and could address more supportively the cares, concerns, and joys of their existence as black people.

Total institutional independence may not have come had white clergy and church officials not continued their rude, paternalistic control even in these separate congregations. But they did, and blacks decided that it was better to step out permanently on their own than to endure this kind of treatment.

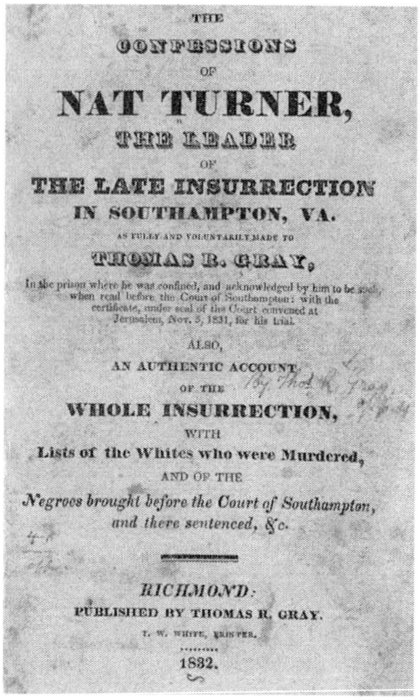

THE
CONFESSIONS
OF
NAT TURNER,
THE LEADER
OF
THE LATE INSURRECTION
IN SOUTHAMPTON, VA.
AS FULLY AND VOLUNTARILY MADE TO
THOMAS R. GRAY,
In the prison where he was confined, and acknowledged by him to be such, when read before the Court of Southampton: with the certificate, under seal of the Court convened at Jerusalem, Nov. 5, 1831, for his trial.
ALSO,
AN AUTHENTIC ACCOUNT
OF THE
WHOLE INSURRECTION,
WITH
Lists of the Whites who were Murdered,
AND OF THE
Negroes brought before the Court of Southampton, and there sentenced, &c.

RICHMOND:
PUBLISHED BY THOMAS R. GRAY.
T. W. WHITE, PRINTER.
1832.

Words of revolution
While in prison, Nat Turner dictated the details of his life and his revolt to South Carolina doctor Thomas Gray, who later published the result as The Confessions of Nat Turner. *The book remains an important record of early life for African Americans.*

The new independent denominations did well in attracting members, and over the decades, additional black-led denominations formed. In 1870, following the Civil War, most of the black members of the Methodist Episcopal Church, South, were set up by that body as the Colored (later Christian) Methodist Episcopal (CME) Church. A decade later, in 1880, black Baptists began the coalition of congregations and regional associations that later became the National Baptist Convention, USA, Inc. Several other Baptist denominational bodies would follow. And in 1897, the Revs. Charles Price Jones (1865–1949) and Charles Harrison Mason (1866–1961) led in the formation of the Pentecostal/Holiness denomination named the Church of God in Christ.

At the same time, some blacks remained members of the white-controlled church bodies, choosing to work for justice and inclusiveness from within rather than seeking relief in alternative structures.

The Case of Nat Turner

It may seem strange to connect church growth with Nat Turner (1800–1831), a relatively short-lived insurrectionist who never ranged far from the place of his birth, and who was executed at the age of 31. But in a negative way, this connection is historically crucial. Turner was born on the Turner plantation of Southampton County, Virginia. As a young man he developed an intense devotional life, given much to prayer and fasting (withholding food from oneself for spiritual reasons), and he became a frequent plantation preacher. When he was 25, he began having visions of blood on plants and strange inscriptions on leaves; these fed his sense that he had a great, divinely ordained mission in life. An 1828 vision revealed to him what that mission was: to liberate African Americans from slavery.

Turner interpreted the solar eclipse of 1831 as a sign that God was signaling that his mission be carried out. Gathering followers and devising a strategy, Turner launched a revolt on August 22, 1831. Starting with the Travis home, in which he now lived, his troops attacked whites in various sections of Southampton County over the next two days. But they were overcome by the white police forces. Those taken captive were tried and 17 were hanged. Turner managed to avoid capture for some two months, but was finally brought in. He was tried and executed in the city of Jerusalem, the ironically named county seat of

Southampton County. When his interrogators tried to coax a confession of wrongdoing from him, his only reply was, "Was not Jesus crucified?"

Turner's revolt, in which about 60 whites were killed, struck fear in the hearts of Southerners, not to mention retaliatory anger that resulted in the revenge killing of dozens of blacks. This was not the first major slave revolt, but it was the most extensive and costly in white lives. It intensified the anxieties about Northerners who lived in the South, especially blacks and those known to hold abolitionist sentiments (a belief that slavery should be abolished, or done away with). Civil authorities, in fact, instituted "black codes," which were laws prohibiting or carefully controlling black movement and activities.

Consequently, the black denominations that had recently formed and which saw a fertile field of evangelism in the millions of enslaved were essentially cut off from this group. The prospects for the growth of their ministries were thus limited to the small minority of blacks living in the North and the people they might encounter in overseas missions.

Northern white missionaries were similarly restricted. Southern white church leaders, on the other hand, stepped up their outreach to blacks and did bring large numbers into church membership. This partly seems to have been to counter the accusation from the North that the Southern churches were ignoring their Christian duty and abandoning millions of black souls to spiritual ignorance in order to protect the economic interests of the slavery system. Energetic efforts at slave evangelism were made, even though the gospel that was preached to them was geared to serve slavery. The typical scriptural text used for slave sermons was Ephesians 6:5: "Servants, be obedient to your masters . . . as unto Christ." As we saw in the discussion earlier in this chapter about slave worship, though, the enslaved often were able to perceive a more affirming, non-submissive message of "good news" in the gospel they heard.

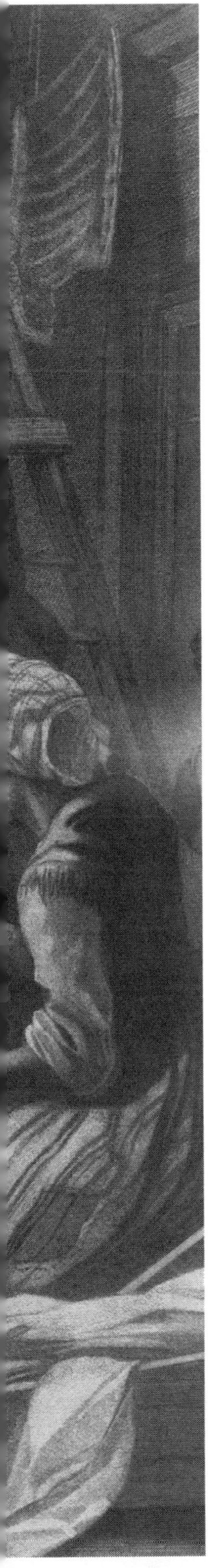

2

Important African-American Events

IN THE HISTORY OF AFRICAN-AMERICAN RELIGION IN THE UNITED States, there are numerous events that have shaped the narrative of church life for African-Americans. We will examine just a few of them here.

"To Set the Captives Free": Emancipation

On January 1, 1863, the Emancipation Proclamation, freeing all slaves in the Confederate states, went into effect. The document was signed by President Abraham Lincoln (1809–1865) to help the Union in the ongoing Civil War, but it had a galvanizing effect on African Americans, too. Many black Christians used Biblical images to describe what was taking place. Some called it the Year of Jubilee, referring to the instruction in the book of Deuteronomy that periodically all slaves be freed and all debts forgiven. Others compared it to the deliverance of the Israelites from Egypt or from Babylonian captivity.

To many black Christians, who deeply believed that God was committed to redeeming the oppressed and bringing about the release of innocent captives, emancipation was inevitable. Given this belief, when it did come on January 1, Emancipation Day became a holiday celebrated in the churches (even into the late 20th century in some places.) It was the confirmation of an article of their faith, the demonstration of who African-American

WORDS OF FREEDOM

Here are the opening lines of the Emancipation Proclamation, issued by President Abraham Lincoln.

That on the 1st day of January, A.D. 1863, all persons held as slaves within any State or designated part of a State the people whereof shall then be in rebellion against the United States [that is, the Confederate states] shall be then, thenceforward, and forever free; and the executive government of the United States, including the military and naval authority thereof, will recognize and maintain the freedom of such persons and will do no act or acts to repress such persons, or any of them, in any efforts they may make for their actual freedom.

PRECEDING PAGE

And now you're free . . . *The life-changing impact of the 1863 Emancipation Proclamation is shown in the faces of these slaves in this 1864 engraving by J.W. Watts.*

Christians believed God to be. It called for sacred ceremonies of thanksgiving and devotion for this divine act of social salvation.

Emancipation had another direct impact on African-American church life. The South, where the great majority of blacks lived, had always been wary of Northern blacks. The presence of free blacks was a dangerous symbol in a system of racial slavery. And since black preachers might (and often did) pick up on and advance the parts of Christian thought that called for equality and liberty, they and the churches they represented were particularly to be barred from slavery's environs. But with emancipation, all that changed. Neither law nor local practice could hold back the newly freed black millions from embracing their faith. And so, missionaries from the black denominations moved into the South with great energy. In many cases the Union armies turned over church buildings in the liberated areas to the possession of these black churches.

The newly freed men and women of the South took great delight in the concept of national black religious organizations that matched those of the ruling white class. To affiliate with such organizations was an exciting, deeply satisfying prospect. And so emancipated blacks left the "invisible institution" as well as the established white-led denominational churches and joined these black faith communities. It was partly in response to this turn of events that the Methodist Episcopal Church, South, cooperated at the time of emancipation in setting up their black members as the Colored (Christian) Methodist Episcopal Church. The effect of this emancipation-related shift in black church fortunes was so dramatic that within 25 years the membership in the black denominations had quadrupled.

Another Place—a Better Life

Around 1910 there began the stirrings of what was soon to become the largest internal population migration the nation had ever experienced. Millions of African Americans moved from the rural South to the urban North in search of work and, they hoped, better lives. This mass movement of people had a dramatic impact on many faith communities, which traveled north right along with the workers.

There were a number of reasons for this population shift. Following the Civil War, most blacks remained in the South. Even though it had been the place of their enslavement, it seemed the logical place to be. They hoped to use their agricultural skills to build a new life under freedom. But the federal government handled emancipation and Reconstruction poorly. It did not provide protection against the re-establishment of abusive Southern white control over blacks, nor did it provide a financial head start to the deprived former slaves.

With neither protection, nor land, nor any other resources, blacks found themselves at the mercy of the white population that had so recently fought to hold them in the status of legal property. As a result, most became trapped in a system of sharecropping and tenant farming, working and living on white-owned property in exchange for a share of what they produced. The terms of these agreements, set by the landowners, so heavily favored the owners that in good years blacks simply made ends meet, while in bad years they fell into ever-increasing debt. Those blacks who hired themselves out as laborers were always subject to unethical white employers who could manipulate wages and working conditions without legal penalty.

Further, governing bodies across the South enacted Jim Crow laws that severely limited black freedom and social prerogatives, enforcing the laws by brutal violence against those who stepped beyond their "place." Slowly, blacks began abandoning the rural South for urban areas, especially in the North. The initial trickle of migration became a mass exit by the early years of World War I (1914–1918). Floods and boll weevil infestation were devastating Southern crops, thus crumbling blacks' already unstable economic foundations.

At the same time, the outbreak of the war placed a severe limitation on European immigration, interrupting the supply of labor on which Northern industry traditionally depended. The crisis for industry was heightened by the increased production demands generated by the war effort. Steel mills, factories, and packing houses decided to send labor recruiters to the South to entice black workers to come North. Some dispensed free railroad tickets to those who accepted a job offer, while others sent trucks to immediately transport their recruits. The circumstances of black life in the South combined with the new employment opportunities to open the gates for migration. Savings were accumulated, possessions were sold, and tickets purchased for the journey North.

Several cities became popular destinations for the migrants. Following the major rail and highway routes, one route of migration

RECONSTRUCTION

This was the name of the period in American history following the Civil War, during which the nation worked to rebuild the South, damaged by years of conflict.

JIM CROW LAWS

Jim Crow laws, named for a minstrel show character, were late-19th-century rules and regulations passed by the legislatures of Southern states. Because of these laws, blacks and whites could not ride together in the same railroad cars, sit in the same waiting rooms, use the same bathrooms, eat in the same restaurants, or sit in the same theaters. Blacks were denied access to parks, beaches, and picnic areas; they were barred from many hospitals.

The laws were slowly erased beginning after World War II, and the Civil Rights movement of the 1960s helped eliminate all of them.

To the Promised Land

As the image of the North filtered south through the promises of agents, the glowing letters of friends, and the appeals of the Negro press, it took on a mythical quality that gave an almost religious significance to the migration. Much of the language used to encourage migration was highly charged with Biblical imagery: the Flight out of Egypt; Bound for the Promised land; Going into Canaan; Beulah Land. A party of migrants on their way from Mississippi to Chicago held solemn ceremonies when their train crossed the Ohio River; they stopped their watches, knelt down to pray, and sang the gospel hymn, "I Done Come Out of the Land of Egypt with the Good News."

The story of ancient Israel's exodus from Egypt, as told in the Hebrew scriptures, had long served in American thought as the model for how God acted for "his people's benefit" in American history. Each successful stage of the nation's development was understood to be a modern version of that model. As African Americans adopted the Judeo-Christian heritage and came to view the circumstances of their life through its lens, they, too, saw the Exodus story as a model for their historical experience. As one Negro spiritual phrased it, "The God that lived in Moses' time is still the same today."

More than one champion of black rights and dignity over the years came to be called a "Moses." Martin Luther King, Jr. (1929–1968) touched deep-flowing streams of recognition and response when he used the images of Moses from Exodus to declare in a famous 1963 speech that "I have been to the mountaintop; I've seen the Promised Land . . . . and we as a people will get to the Promised Land." It was in this way of thinking and, for some, this faith understanding, that Southern blacks made their hopeful way North. It gave a stamp of divine support to their move; it intensified the desire to seek what lay ahead.

ran along the Eastern seaboard to such cities as Philadelphia, Newark, New York, and Hartford. Another route went through the Southwestern states and into California. The cities of the Midwest were the goal of still other routes.

Those migrants who arrived in the North and found their expectations fulfilled wrote to those down South and encouraged them to make the journey. They praised the comparative social freedom of Northern life and its benefits, including better schools, better health care, and, especially, plentiful, high-paying employment. Many letters stressed that up North employers paid what they had agreed to pay, which, sadly, was not common practice in the South.

In editorial after editorial, the *Chicago Defender*, a black-owned newspaper with national influence, vigorously promoted migration. It urged the black man "for the sake of his wife and children to leave every spot in the south [sic] where his worth is not appreciated enough to give him the standing of a man and a citizen in the community."

Indeed, it offered May 15, 1917, as the informal inauguration date for what it termed the "Great Northern Drive."

A Case Study of the Churches and Migration: Chicago

The black churches of Chicago saw the migration as both a challenge and an opportunity. They shared the *Defender*'s encouragement of black migration; as the migrants arrived, they stepped forward to help out. Some congregations sent welcoming committees to the transportation depots to greet the travelers and assist them in finding lodging and necessary services. They also extended invitations to their places of worship. For awhile, messages of invitation were published in the *Defender* every week.

Several congregations already had social service programs, such as employment and housing bureaus. These now were expanded and made available to the migrants. Worship services, too, might be altered to accommodate the accustomed worship styles of the migrants. The churches provided much-needed and deeply appreciated support

Some Telling Numbers

The statistical picture of the migration is striking. In 1890 Chicago's black population was 14,271. By 1910 the number had risen to 44,103. But the figure for 1920 was 109,458, an increase of some 148 percent in that first decade of full-blown migration, with most of it occurring between 1916 and 1920. The next 10 years added another 124,445 African Americans to Chicago's population.

This is our place

In this 1903 photo, Rev. R.C. Ransom and his wife are shown on the steps of the Institutional AME Church on Dearborn Street in Chicago. It was one of many churches that boomed in the early 1900s following a large migration of African Americans from the South.

for people who often had very limited resources and little comprehension of how to manage life in the urban North.

One result for the Northern churches was a swelling of their membership, in some cases doubling, even tripling their pre-migration numbers by 1919. For example, Bethel African Methodist Episcopal took in 650 new members; South Park Methodist Episcopal, 2,425. Olivet Baptist, alone, added more than 5,000, for a total membership of nearly 10,000, making it reportedly the largest Protestant congregation in the world. Those churches most active in welcoming the migrants and addressing their concerns gained the most new members. Because there was not enough space in existing church buildings for the actual and potential new members, buildings were expanded and new ones constructed. In 1912, there were 28 black congregations among the various denominations. By 1919, there were 147.

But both the migrants and the churches faced adjustment issues. The migrants were accustomed to churches with small congregations and small buildings. Many found the large city churches overwhelming. Similarly, relationships in Southern rural churches were face-to-face; each person was known intimately and participation in the life of the church was acknowledged and affirmed. These were not the traditions of the urban North. Even had they been, new arrivals, as outsiders in many ways, could not expect to move easily and quickly into established circles of friendship and structures of church operation. Also, worship in the South tended to be informal and much more freely expressive than had come to be the case in the North.

Earlier black settlers in Chicago had left behind much of the style and content of their Southern rural worship heritage, developing their own sort of worship style that was less spontaneous and more subdued and decorous.

One should not conclude that all Chicago pastors disallowed emotive, expressive worship, nor that all rural Southerners worshiped that way. Clearly, though, on the whole, the black urban church in the North, in its size, its style of church order, and its ways of worship, reflected changes that had taken place in American Protestantism in general after the mid-19th century, as the frontier was subdued and the nation became more urbanized. Black Northern churches functioned in a way that many migrants to the city experienced as different, at best, and, at worst, unsatisfying.

African-American Jews

The number of African-Americans among the 5 million Jewish people in America is a tiny minority; most estimates are less than 200,000. In many cases, the people are products of marriage between a black person and a white Jewish person. Since Jewish heritage passes through the mother, this is often a Jewish woman.

The Alliance of Black Jews was founded in 1995 by Robin Washington, a Boston-area newspaper editor. The group holds informational forums for African-American Jews, and works with other Jewish groups.

Several African-American celebrities are Jewish, including actor Yaphet Kotto, actress Lisa Bonet, musician Lenny Kravitz, and author Walter Mosley. The late actor-singer Sammy Davis, Jr., was perhaps the most well-known African-American Jew.

The Firm Establishment of Islam

Islam had been practiced by some enslaved Africans since their early days in the United States. It was not until the 20th century, though, that it became widely visible as a part of the religious life of African-Americans. It surfaced under many different leaders and took different organizational forms. Noble Drew Ali (1886–1929) believed that African-Americans were rightly called Moors—descendants of their Moroccan homeland. He believed that their true religion was Islam, not the Christianity that so many had embraced. Ali advanced his version of Islam, which he named Moorish Science, from the Moorish Science Temple of America, established in 1913. He published his beliefs in *The Holy Koran* (which is a different book from the Qur'an of mainstream Islam).

The Nation of Islam was begun in 1933 by a follower of Noble Drew Ali, Wallace Fard Muhammad (1877–1934). One of Muhammad's recruits, Elijah Poole, changed his name to Elijah Muhammad (1897–1975), and was the engine for the Nation's early growth. Born in

Forging Alternatives

Here are two of perhaps hundreds of stories which can be told of the encounters between migrants and Chicago's established black churches.

The late Rev. Hazelia Savage once told the author of this book about her aunt. Mary Butler, who in 1922 sought permission from the pastor of her church, St. Stephen AME, to conduct services for migrant members of the congregation who felt too embarrassed by their meager wardrobe to attend Sunday worship. Permission granted, the group was established and sustained under Butler's leadership, meeting first in her home, then in rented quarters. Ultimately, it was organized into a separate church, called the Mary Butler AME Church. It still serves a small, devoted congregation on Chicago's West Side.

In another narrative, recounted by researcher Allan Spear, Lucy Smith came to Chicago from Atlanta in 1910. When she attended prominent local Baptist churches, she found herself very uncomfortable with the formal style of worship. But in a Pentecostal church community, she received personal fulfillment and also a calling to be in religious leadership.

By 1916, she had begun inviting other migrants to prayer meetings in her home. Relocating through several rented properties, Elder Lucy Smith finally gathered the resources to erect her own building and went on to extend a vital ministry, largely to the socially marginalized residents of the South Side.

Georgia, Poole and his wife, Clara, had come to Detroit in 1923. There he began to follow Muhammad and joined his new Temple No. 1 of the Nation of Islam. Poole rose to become Muhammad's lieutenant, and having given himself the surname Muhammad, went to Chicago in 1932 to establish a second temple there. After Wallace Muhammad's mysterious disappearance in 1934, Elijah Muhammad emerged as the new leader of the movement, which he headquartered in Chicago.

The movement experienced what seemed to be a setback in 1942 when Elijah Muhammad was arrested, supposedly for remarks he had made that were sympathetic to the Japanese, with whom the United States was at war. While acquitted of the charges, he was eventually jailed for draft evasion, though he was 45 years old. But after four years of imprisonment on these charges, his status as a leader of the Nation of Islam was even higher than before.

Muhammad taught a message of pride in black heritage. He encouraged members to reject their European last names, which had typically been taken from a slaveowner's family name, and adopt either a Muslim name or an X, representing their unknown true family name. He emphasized healthy, respectable lifestyles and healthy dietary habits, and published a book called *How to Eat to Live*. He called for blacks to strive to be economically independent from whites by establishing their own businesses. The Nation of Islam set the example by operating a large farm in Michigan and several small business enterprises.

This kind of racial advocacy, centered around Elijah Muhammad as the "Messenger of Allah," caused some to characterize the group's version of Islam as unorthodox and in conflict with Islam's racial inclusiveness and the authority of the original prophet Muhammad. Elijah Muhammad always argued that his was a legitimate Islam, one among the many varieties of Islam within the Muslim family.

If Elijah Muhammad firmly fixed a place for Islam in the African-American community, it was one of his recruits who was the spark for the tremendous growth and geographic spread of the Nation through the 1950s and '60s. Malcolm Little (1925–1965), better known by his adopted name of Malcolm X, was a fiery orator whose in-your-face style of racial analysis and social criticism captivated black audiences and terrified whites. His father was a minister and an outspoken civil rights advocate, but Malcolm drifted into street crime, resulting eventually in his incarceration for armed robbery and assault.

Different Worship Styles

Religious studies historian James Richard Grossman wrote in his 1982 doctoral thesis at the University of California at Berkeley:

Migrants were accustomed to services accompanied by improvisational singing, shouting, and other forms of active participation and demonstrated enthusiasm. These men and women hardly enjoyed the intellectual sermons of such men as Rev. William Braddan of Berean Baptist Church, who refused to hold revivals and prohibited standing in his church during services. Even at such places as Walters AME Zion, where migrants apparently worshiped as they pleased, they could hardly be unaware that the pastor, Rev. W.A. Blackwell, considered "singing, shouting, and talking being the most useless ways of proving Christianity."

Drawing a crowd
A fiery and dynamic speaker, Malcolm X brought African-American Islam much more strongly into the national picture. He mixed a message of faith and social change that inspired many black Americans in the 1960s.

Converted to the Nation of Islam while in prison, he put his street savvy and his keen intellect into the service of his passion for justice and equity for black people. Because he was loyal to the claims of truth as he understood it, above the claims of authority or the threats of power, he challenged wrong wherever he believed it to exist, even up to the highest ranks of the Nation itself. In so doing, he fell into disfavor with the Nation's leadership.

By 1964, he had broken with the Nation of Islam and formed two organizations: the Muslim Mosque, Inc., and the Organization of Afro-American Unity. The former was based in Islam, the latter was non-religious, but both had in their focus the elimination of black oppression. On February 21, 1965, Malcolm X was assassinated while delivering a public address in Harlem, New York. Three members of the Nation of Islam were convicted of his murder in 1966.

Malcolm X's assassination only magnified his fame and drew many more to study his ideas. His autobiography, published posthumously (and co-written with Alex Hailey, later to become famous as the author of *Roots*), became a bestseller. He remains today a powerful symbol of courageous, informed social criticism to bring about social change.

Meanwhile, the Nation of Islam continued to grow under Elijah Muhammad's leadership. Effective recruitment was done in the neighborhoods and in prisons, where startling success was achieved in reforming convicts' lives and setting them on a productive path. The Nation's message was spread, among other ways, through the weekly publication *Muhammad Speaks*, sold on street corners by the familiar well-dressed, bow-tied recruits. By the time of Elijah Muhammad's death in 1975, the Nation of Islam counted some 100,000 men and women in its membership.

SPEAKING IN TONGUES

Also called "glossolalia," this term applies to people who are filled with the Holy Spirit. They speak in a language that is not necessarily understood by those around them, and are thought to be inspired by the Holy Spirit.

William Seymour and the Azusa Street Revival

The Holiness/Pentecostal churches make up one of the largest segments of U.S. Protestantism. They owe much of their place in popular acceptance to the phenomenon created by the famed Azusa Street Revival campaign launched by William Joseph Seymour (1870–1922).

Seymour was born in Louisiana. As a young man, he affiliated first with the Methodist Church then the Church of God in Anderson, Indiana. In 1905, he heard the teachings of Charles F. Parham (1873–1929), who helped develop Pentecostalism. The next year saw Seymour in Los Angeles, serving as the pastor of a black Holiness congregation.

Influence beyond L.A. *Though he started his ministry in Los Angeles, "Holiness" preacher William Seymour's influence spread nationwide among both black and white congregations.*

However, the congregation eventually locked him out because of his Pentecostal teachings. Not discouraged, Seymour continued his ministry through a series of prayer meetings.

In one of these meetings, people began speaking in tongues, which Holiness doctrine says is the sign of the "baptism of the Holy Spirit," and is expected of all believers. This event was the beginning of a revival. More and more people began turning out to participate in this new spiritual experience.

The increasing numbers meant the need for a larger meeting space, so a former church building on Azusa Street was rented. The local attendees were a mixed group of white, Hispanic, and black persons. With the publication of a periodical and the ordination of other ministers, word of the revival spread to other states. Soon the movement drew to Los Angeles a stream of people of all races from around the country and overseas, while new congregations were forming nationally. The mother institution was called the Azusa Street Apostolic Faith Mission of Los Angeles.

Beginning in 1908, Seymour and the Azusa Street Mission experienced a number of setbacks, including both racial and doctrinal disputes within the organization. As a result, this movement, which sparked and sponsored many significant and long-lasting denominational developments, began a steep decline that it was never able fully to reverse.

One significant black church figure influenced by the revival was the Rev. Charles H. Mason (1866–1961) of Tennessee. In 1907 Mason was among the many visitors to the Azusa Street Revival, where he experienced the "baptism of the Holy Spirit," confirmed by speaking in tongues. He and the Rev. Charles Price Jones co-founded the Church of God in Christ in 1907.

HOLINESS AND PENTECOSTALISM

The Holiness strain of Protestantism first developed in America in the 1870s. The belief was that it was the duty of Christians to seek after what was called holiness, or a "sanctified" life. Many Holiness churches emphasize behavior, that is, acting the part of a person of Christ. In those early days, several Holiness churches split off from Methodism.

Another group that split off during the early 20th century were the Pentecostals, who preached that a person should have a physical, spiritual, intense experience of the Holy Spirit. The movement's name is from the event in the Bible called Pentecost, when the Holy Spirit was given to Jesus' apostles after his death.

Both white and African-American congregations of various types embraced one or the other of these forms of belief and worship.

The Civil Rights Movement

The theme of liberation for human beings has always been central to the African-American concept of faith. It could be seen in each of the keystone events we have examined thus far—the drive toward independent churches; migration to a "Promised Land"; forms of Islam that spoke specifically to the black social condition; and new ways of understanding God's spirit that empowered people to live in hope even when their circumstances were grim. Of the hundreds of organized slave revolts that occurred between 1619 and 1860, many were either led by preachers or were understood by their participants to be expressions of God's will.

Whether under religious leadership and motivations or not, African-American efforts to achieve legal protections and legal and political rights were continuous. There was not always agreement on how to pursue those goals. For instance, the well-known educator and social leader Booker T. Washington (1856–1915) believed that hard work and respectable behavior would convince whites that blacks should be given citizen's rights. Scholar and social activist W.E.B. Dubois (1868–1963) disagreed. He believed that direct social and political action were necessary to pressure government and social structures into giving blacks their rights. So it was not a new development when, in the mid-20th century, this stream of thought took shape in a national Civil Rights movement with clear and open religious overtones.

A Key Decision

In 1954, the Supreme Court essentially ruled that creating separate schools for black and white children was illegal. The case they ruled on was called Brown vs. Board of Education. The "Brown" of that case was a minister, the Rev. Oliver Brown of Topeka, Kansas. Rev. Brown filed suit when his daughter was not allowed to attend an all-white school.

When pioneers of the movement in the South, such as Fannie Lou Hamer (1917–1977), organized blacks to push for their rights, Negro spirituals and familiar religious songs were used to cement group morale and provide encouragement amidst very real danger. The rallies and meetings of the movement typically were held in churches. Those who emerged as leaders of the movement included active religious laypersons such as Rosa Parks, John Lewis, Bayard Rustin, James Farmer, and Pauli Murray. Certainly crucial in leadership were clergy, including Murray, who became an Episcopal priest; Revs. Vernon Johns, Fred Shuttlesworth, Andrew Young, Jesse Jackson, Joseph Lowery, Wyatt Tee Walker, Ralph David Aberathy, and Martin Luther King, Jr.

King was the son and grandson of socially activist clergy, so he had an understanding of ministry that applied the Christian message to life. He shaped and refined that legacy through his own intellectual and spiritual gifts. The result was a vision of inclusive social life in the United States that was, as he said, ". . . deeply rooted in the American dream," while framed by the Judeo-Christian heritage of love and justice (Read more about Martin Luther King, Jr., in chapter 6.)

Today, ministers, along with committed laypersons such as Marian Wright Edelman and Vernon Jarrett, continue work that is now two centuries old. The Civil Rights movement remains a key example of the African-American tradition of blending laypeople and ordained ministry with work toward social justice for all.

Describing Black Theology for All

In 1969, James Hal Cone (b.1938), a young AME minister from Bearden, Arkansas, published his doctoral thesis and reshaped the field of religious studies and the way that theology is taught. Cone was concerned about issues of racial injustice and oppression, which he had experienced firsthand, and took this as the focus of his studies. He wanted to show how the theology of the church had, in fact, supported and advanced the enslavement of Africans and the racial abuse that was so contrary to the gospel the church proclaimed. He was concerned with what he called the "theological blindness of white professors in relation to black oppression." He wanted to answer the question, "What has the gospel to do with blacks in their struggle for liberation?"

Cone's doctoral thesis pulled together his research and reflection on these matters. It was published in 1969 under the title *Black Theology and Black Power*. He was not the first to relate the gospel to the black struggle. Black clergy and laity had been doing so throughout the time of slavery and beyond, in sermons, speeches, and written documents of many types. David Walker's "Appeal" is an early 19th-century example. However, Cone was the first to publish extended, formal theological reflection on the subject and the first on record to use the term "Black Theology" to name this arena of thought and speech.

Initially, white theologians ignored this bold approach to theology. They declared that there was nothing in black religious thought that was worthy of serious study. But the increasing intensity of the Civil Rights movement of the 1960s and '70s, pressing upon all social institutions, including church and academia, forced a greater willingness to hear Black Theology's message and to take it seriously. This was especially helped by the pressure black students and faculty placed upon seminaries and schools of theology to incorporate black presence and concerns in the lessons and staffing of these institutions.

Cone's bold initiative has both opened the way for and sparked the construction of other new types of theology, such as Feminist Theology, Womanist Theology (concerned with black women), and Mujerista Theology (concerned with Latina women). Cone and other black theologians have participated in the shaping of movements in other countries, such Liberation Theology in Latin America and the Minjung Theology of Korea. Black Theology is now a well-established part of religious and theological studies.

Another kind of robe
In 1989, Barbara Harris became the first women to be made a bishop of the Episcopal Church. She was one of several African-American women who rose to higher church office in recent years.

Women at the Altar

For nearly 200 years African-American women have stepped forward to proclaim a divine calling into ministry. But for most of Christian history, the ordained ministry, and even the role of preacher, has been reserved exclusively for men. African-American denominations are no exception. In the early 19th century, for example, Jarena Lee, a woman of commanding preaching ability, was never appointed pastor of a church and was only reluctantly allowed to preach. As women increasingly demonstrated their effectiveness as preachers, they were allowed to assume the office of evangelist, a traveling preacher with no church assignment, but still were barred from ordination and the chance to lead a congregation.

Many black women served as missionaries. They served in the many home and foreign missionary societies formed in the African-American denominations in the 19th century. But women continued to press for a fuller recognition of their gifts and commitment to official service in and through the church. Late in the 19th century, the doors opened wider as the offices of stewardess and deaconess were instituted in the Methodist-type churches as official, though unordained, offices. Stewardesses and deaconnesses were commissioned to do works of charity and support women in distressed circumstances and to assist men in certain churchly tasks and liturgical functions.

By century's end, the AME Zion Church had ordained two women, but such events were to be rare for many years to come. The AME Church and the CME Church did not allow full ordination for women until 1948 and 1956, respectively.

A decade later, perhaps inspired by the Civil Rights and feminist movements, women across the country, black and white, began to assert more forcefully their claim to full equality in American society. They challenged male privilege and exclusive male domains of power and decision-making. They began to present themselves as as candidates for leadership positions. At the 1989 meeting of the worldwide Anglican Communion, a parish priest, the Rev. Barbara Harris (b.1930), was made its first female bishop. In 1984, the United Methodist Church elected the Rev. Leontyne Kelly (b.1920) as that denomination's second female bishop.

Then, in July, 2000, the General Conference of the African Methodist Episcopal Church elected a 53-year-old pastor from Baltimore, the Rev. Vashti Murphy McKenzie, to the episcopacy. This was the first time an historically black denomination had elevated a woman to the highest office in the church's governing structure.

Bishop McKenzie (pictured on the cover in a purple robe) has written about the accomplishments of women in various societies. She sees her tradition-breaking election as, in part, a vindication of the gifts of those women. It is also, in part, a reflection of the evolution of values and social consciousness of contemporary American society.

HARRISON RHODES MEMORIAL
SOCIAL SCIENCE BUILDING

3

African America: Faith and Culture

WE HAVE SEEN HOW AFRICAN-AMERICAN TRADITIONS HAVE AFFECTED the practice and makeup of their churches. But the effect of those traditions has gone beyond the shaping of congregations, churches, and faith traditions and moved into the wider realm of American life. In American culture, African-American religions have had major impacts in the areas of education, art, literature, and music.

Education

Education has always been highly valued by African Americans. Though education was forbidden for the enslaved in early America—that is, for most African Americans—it was greatly desired, particularly because education, at least literacy, enabled one to read and understand sacred literature. Many slave Christians longed to be able to read so they could read the Bible for themselves. The discovery of portions of the Qur'an among Muslim slave belongings shows the importance of literacy for that small but persistent religious group. And beyond their devotional uses, reading and writing skills could aid in keeping abreast of what was happening in the larger white world, as well as in communicating among the enslaved in pursuit of their own purposes.

LORD OF THE DANCE

In 1960, African-American dancer and choreographer Alvin Ailey (1931–1989) created one of modern dance's most acclaimed works. "Revelations" drew on Ailey's childhood memories of life in the Baptist church, where he worshiped and sang. The dance brought elements of the ceremonies and celebrations in the churches of his youth, and his interpretation of them into dance remains a classic. Critics praised Ailey for bringing his faith so deeply and so beautifully into his art.

Ailey remained among dance's most important artists, and his world-renowned dance company continues to perform "Revelations" in its repertoire.

PRECEDING PAGE

College life

Bethune-Cookman College in Daytona Beach, Florida, is one of many institutions of higher learning founded, run, and attended primarily by African Americans.

The free black population also labored under severe restrictions upon their access to educational opportunities. But whatever learning they acquired enabled them to share in a common identity as American citizens, while aiding in the formation and management of their own institutions, including religious institutions.

The 19th century saw the establishment of several African-American denominational bodies. These organizations, especially the Methodist ones, placed increasing emphasis on educational preparation for the clergy, both as a means to a broader, deeper understanding of the Bible and the church's theology and also to increase the competency of the clergy to fulfill their roles. There were, however, a significant number of clergy and laity who feared that education could quench the spiritual fervor of one's religion, that vital faith did not require "book learning." Yet, as the century progressed, education was seen more and more in the general society as important to full citizenship.

All of the historically black denominations established an assortment of schools, from grammar level through college. Compulsory public education was not universal in the early 19th century. But even as it became so, blacks were typically not allowed to attend the community schools, nor were they provided with separate facilities. So black clergy and churches took up the challenge. They lobbied the public school boards to permit black enrollment. At the same time, they worked with others in the community to provide educational opportunities. They opened schools for black students in black church buildings. Frequently, ministers served as principals and teachers until other staff could be recruited. The Sunday schools common in the black churches also provided training in literacy, organizational leadership, and personal development.

During the period of Reconstruction following the Civil War, one of the most important steps taken by the Southern state legislatures, which were then comprised heavily of black clergy and lay members, was the establishment of a system of free public education.

As public education across the country opened up to black students, clergy were strong in encouraging young people to attend the schools. Many would visit the schools and become acquainted with the teachers, giving their support to the educational process, as well as establishing a point of accountability for both teachers and learners.

And there were further connections between school and church. Often the teachers and principals who were in charge Monday through Friday acted again as Sunday school teachers and superintendents. At marking periods, some clergy would have their student members bring their report cards to church, for praise or encouragement, as needed.

On other fronts, clergy fostered education through the establishment of training institutes for clergy and laity. They have continued in the precedent of lobbying for adequate public school facilities to serve black students and for quality educational programs in existing schools. Many have served on local school boards so that they can directly affect education in their communities.

The Performing Arts

Until their final elimination in the 1960s, a variety of local laws prevented African Americans from going into theaters, concert halls, or various other public or private places of performance and entertainment. Consequently, the black church again stepped in to fill the void. Here, one's talents—musical, oratorical, literary, dramatic, and otherwise—were encouraged, refined, and given opportunity for expres-

Mary McLeod Bethune

One of the most important educators of the 20th century was Mary McLeod Bethune. Born in 1875 as one of 17 children, she realized early on that education was the key to improving her life. She studied at a seminary in North Carolina and later at the Moody Bible Institute. After several teaching posts, she moved with her family to Palatka, Florida.

The small school she started in 1904 grew quickly and in 1923 became Bethune-Cookman College. Bethune also became very involved in the voting rights movement, inspiring hundreds of African Americans to take advantage of their rights, especially helping women to vote following passage of the 19th Amendment in 1920.

Her reputation grew in the 1920s and she became one of the nation's most prominent African-American citizens. Bethune was appointed to many presidential and government commissions on education, employment, and race relations, and was especially influential in the administration of President Franklin Roosevelt, owing to a friendship with Eleanor Roosevelt, the president's wife. In 1936, Bethune became the first black person to head a national agency, when she took over part of the National Youth Administration.

She remained an important figure on the national scene, a testament to the power of education and perseverance. Bethune died in 1955.

sion. Sunday schools provided regular occasions for recitation and public speaking. This was extended in oratorical contests, staged debates, or the leadership of worship, including preaching, on Youth Sundays. The choir loft during Sunday worship or the recurrent Sunday afternoon musicals were the concert stage for the developing vocalist, to say nothing of the training afforded the accompanying musicians. Christmas pageants, Easter programs, and other celebrations provided the venues for a range of dramatists- and artists-in-training.

As informal as these venues may seem, they must not be taken lightly. Outside of the church and schools, there was virtually no other place where gifted African Americans were allowed to receive, or could afford to receive, the inspiration, nurture, and practice by which artistry could come to bloom and be recognized. There are hardly any acclaimed African-American performing artists, past or present, in either classical or popular arts, who do not trace their foundations to their early years in the black church.

Visual and Literary Arts

The impact of African-American religion on the other branches of art is of a somewhat different but related type. The African-American religious experience, especially as filtered through the teachings and the organizational life of the black church, has been the inspiration for many black visual artists and composers. But their artistic productions are not usually developed and rehearsed or performed in the church setting. Rather, they are informed and inspired by the artists' experiences in the church. Typically, their works are not devotional materials or specifically about the church, itself. They span the range of human issues, relationships, struggles, challenges, and triumphs, but are guided by religious insights and values, or draw upon aspects of the black church as a backdrop for their message.

Some of the works of 18th-century black poets such as Phillis Wheatley and Jupiter Hammon incorporated orthodox religious language, though with little reference to racial concerns. Nineteenth-century poet George McClellan (1860–1934) ends his 1916 verse about Christ's compassion ("The Path of Dreams") with a reference to those who "have felt the wrong of trampled rights, of caste" (caste is another word for regimented social class). Internationally renowned 19th-cen-

Litany at Atlanta

Here is an excerpt from W.E.B. DuBois' *Litany at Atlanta.*

Bewildered we are, and passion-tost, mad with the madness of a mobbed and mocked and murdered people, straining at the armposts of Thy Throne, we raise our shackled hands and charge Thee, God, by the bones of our stolen fathers, by the tears of our dead mothers, by the very blood of Thy crucified Christ: What meaneth this? Tell us the Plan; give us the Sign!

Keep not thou silence, O God!

Sit no longer blind, Lord God, deaf to our prayer and dumb to our dumb suffering. Surely Thou too art not white, O Lord, a pale, bloodless, heartless thing?

Ah! Christ of all the pities!

Renaissance man
W.E.B. DuBois was one of the most influential African Americans of the 20th century. He was a writer, teacher, and forceful activist for equal rights for blacks.

tury painter Benjamin O. Tanner (1775–1848) was the son of an AME bishop. His works are often striking interpretations of Biblical images.

Just after the turn of the 20th century, scholar and civil rights journalist W.E.B. DuBois (1868–1963) published the poem *A Litany at Atlanta*. Written in response to a deadly rampage of whites through Atlanta's black community in 1906, it was a bold complaint against the seeming silence and inattention of God and a poignant plea to God for justice and protective intervention against a murderous white onslaught.

Among his many contributions to civil rights, in 1905, DuBois led in the formation of the Niagara Movement, the organization that

An Important Song

Here is the first verse of "Lift Ev'ry Voice and Sing":

Lift every voice and sing
Till earth and heaven ring,
Ring with the harmonies of Liberty;
Let our rejoicing rise
High as the listening skies,
Let it resound loud as the rolling sea.
Sing a song full of the faith that the dark past has taught us,
Sing a song full of the hope that the present has brought us,
Facing the rising sun of our new day begun,
Let us march on till victory is won.

eventually became the National Association for the Advancement of Colored People—the NAACP—which remains today a vital force for the rights of African Americans.

James Weldon Johnson's book *God's Trombones*, published in 1927, celebrates the power and artistry of black preaching as Johnson (1871–1938) cast in verse form some of the classic sermons he had heard over the years. But Johnson's best known work, which he composed with his brother, J. Rosamond, in 1900, is "Lift Ev'ry Voice and Sing," a rousing semi-patriotic song which recalls the bloody, brutal 300-year experience of Africans transplanted by force to the United States. It speaks of the faith learned from the past, the hope the present has ushered in, and "[God] who hast brought us thus far on the way." It is quintessential black church theology and the song was quickly adopted by blacks as the "Negro National Anthem."

Black novelists and playwrights often set their works in a church or religious family; feature characters who are sustained by their faith or are wrestling with profound theological questions of sin, redemption, grace, or death; level critiques at the perceived inadequacy, irrelevance, or hypocrisy of the black church and its teachings in face of black life issues; or chronicle a title character's social and religious pilgrimage through life. One can find instances among the fictional writing, for example, of Zora Neale Hurston (1891–1960), Richard Wright (1908–1960), James Baldwin (1924–1987), Toni Morrison (b.1931), and Alice Walker (b.1944).

Marketers of Wellness

In more recent years, a new phenomenon has sprung up: that of widely popular black clergy and lay Christians who offer advice on how to achieve spiritual and personal well-being. In each case, these media personalities were nurtured in the African-American religious experience and offer insights which unapologetically convey the values of that background. Yet they do not necessarily ask persons to accept a particular denominational faith or church membership.

The Rev. T.D. Jakes (b.1957) is pastor of the Potter's House Church in Dallas, Texas, which claims 28,000 members. He has published nearly 100 books, workbooks, and audiocassettes, many translated into Spanish. His works guide readers in how they can apply Christian faith to achieve personal fulfillment, reconstruct broken lives, or meet daily challenges with balance and strength. He is a highly regarded, much sought-after public speaker, whose appeal crosses many lines of race, class, gender, and ethnicity.

Much the same may be said of Iyanla Vanzant (b. 1953), who has written such books as *In the Meantime: Finding Yourself, The Love You Want,* and *Until Today: Daily Devotions for Spiritual Growth and Peace of Mind.* Her books are best sellers and she lectures across the country. More widely recognized and highly regarded than either Jakes or Vanzant is Oprah Winfrey (b. 1954), whose television talk show, monthly magazine, movie and television productions, and other media ventures have made her a contemporary phenomenon of public appeal and influence. Her work, however, is not explicitly faith-based, though some of her inspiration comes from her religious upbringing. There are also a number of African-American television evangelists who draw large interracial audiences (see Frederick Price, page 107).

He Started in the Pulpit

James Baldwin was one of the most important writers of the 20th century. The author of such classic works as *Go Tell It on the Mountain, Notes from a Native Son*, and *The Evidence of Things Not Seen* was born in Harlem in 1924. The son of a preacher, Baldwin followed in his father's footsteps, spending three years preaching.

Though he left the pulpit when he was 18 to travel and study, later living in France for most of his life, Baldwin was greatly influenced by the style of his church preaching. The tones and language of some of his work reflect the influence of classic African-American Christian preaching.

Gospel Music

Music that grew out of the African-American experience, whether secular or spiritual, is one of America's chief contributions to world culture. In the 19th century, the music that came to the fore was the Negro spiritual, created by Christian slaves and brought to the world's

Kwanzaa

This holiday, celebrated over the seven days after Christmas, was created in 1966 by Maulana Karenga, a teacher and social activist in California. The word *Kwanzaa* means "first fruits [of the harvest]" in Kiswahili. The seven-day celebration focuses on key elements of life for African descendants, in America and elsewhere. It is not tied to any particular religion, but many African-American families celebrate it along with traditional Christmas events or other religious ceremonies.

On each night of Kwanzaa, celebrants light one of seven candles (three green, three red, and one black, whose colors represent Africa) and talk about one of these seven themes of the holiday (also referred to by Kiswahili names): unity, self-determination, collective work and responsibility, cooperative economics, purpose, creativity, and faith. Readings from modern writers including W.E.B. DuBois and Martin Luther King, Jr., can be included in the ceremony, which also features drinking from a unity cup.

With each drink, the people say "Harambee!" or "Let's all pull together." Other symbols of the holiday and its ceremonies include a straw mat, ears of corn, fruit, and small gifts.

attention through touring choral groups such as the Fisk Jubilee Singers. In the 20th century, black Christianity produced gospel music.

Gospel's roots extend back to the plaintive, powerful spirituals of slavery days and were nurtured in the swing rhythms of turn-of-the- century blues and jazz. The first name associated with gospel is the Rev. Charles A. Tindley (1851–1933), who was pastor of the Tindley Temple Methodist Episcopal Church in Philadelphia. Tindley was a prolific writer of hymns, or church songs for worship, publishing his first collection in 1901. Some of his classic compositions, such as "Stand By Me" and "We'll Understand It Better By and By," are considered as among the first gospel songs.

The person considered the "Father of Gospel" is Thomas Andrew Dorsey (1899–1993). Born in Villa Rica, Georgia, the son of a Baptist minister, Dorsey eventually found his way to Chicago. After studying music at the Chicago Musical College, he went on to establish himself as a popular blues musician. For a time, he was the pianist and bandleader for the famous blues singer Ma Rainey. Eventually, though, Dorsey's music shifted back to his roots in the church, but with a twist. He merged the lyrics of hymns with the rhythms and syncopation of blues. The result was what Dorsey called "gospel music." In 1921 he published his first gospel song, and in 1931 he formed the first gospel choir, at the Ebenezer Baptist Church, Chicago.

Musicologist Portia Maultsby wrote in a 1986 article in the *Journal of the Interdenominational Theology Center*, "Dorsey's blues-based melodies and harmonies, combined with his ragtime, boogie-woogie piano style, captured an urban religious spirit." But if so, it did not immediately capture the urban church audience. Gospel music was not well received at first; many black clergy and church members accused him of "bringing the nightclub into the church." Dorsey, in a sense, did not disagree. In author Lawrence Levine's book *Black Culture and Black Consciousness*, Dorsey said, "I was a blues singer, and I carried that with me into the gospel songs." On another occasion he said, "I started putting a little of the beat into the gospel that we had in jazz."

But for Dorsey, this carryover from blues and jazz to gospel was not casual or by coincidence. He did it with a purpose. Working as he was in the period of the Depression in the 1930s, it was his intention to infuse the "swing" rhythms into gospel so as to help "swing" people out of their troubles. In Levine's book, he said, "I wrote to give them

Stamps of approval
This set of 1998 U.S. postal stamps honors four of the greats of gospel music: Mahalia Jackson, Roberta Martin, Clara Ward, and Sister Rosetta. The stamps were a visible reminder of the music's importance to American culture.

A heavenly voice
Trained from her youth in the music of her Christian church and gospel-singing family, Whitney Houston has used her talents to become a versatile entertainer. She has produced top-selling, award-winning albums of her singing, and has acted in movies and on television.

something to lift them out of that Depression. They could sing at church, but the singing had no life, no spirit . . . . We intended gospel to strike a happy medium for the downtrodden. This music lifted people out of the muck and mire of poverty and loneliness, of being broke, and gave them some kind of hope anyway."

And so he continued to compose and to promote his music, traveling for years with singer Sallie Martin, and later with Mahalia Jackson (1912–1972). Jackson herself was among the first African-American gospel singers to gain widespread success among audiences both in and away from the church.

Meanwhile, Dorsey persisted in spite of rejections, both in the United States and abroad, and gospel music eventually found acceptance. It has been developed and extended by a multitude of composers and performers. Today, it is a standard part of the musical repertoire of Christian churches around the globe, across borders of race and ethnicity. Dorsey's most well-known, well-loved composition, "Precious Lord, Take My Hand," has been translated into 32 languages.

On the Charts

Dorsey's music, combined with the growth of jazz and rhythm and blues, gave rise to a wider spread of gospel music. Singers moved from the choirs to the concert stage, from the churches to the recording studios. Along with Mahalia Jackson's prominence in the 1940s and '50s, other performers made the transition.

Jazz and blues singers Ruth Brown (b.1928) and Aretha Franklin (born in 1942, the daughter of a minister) were among those who achieved international fame with their emotional, powerful talents, using skills first honed singing church music.

More recently, singer and actress Whitney Houston has become one of the music industry's greatest stars. While most of her concerts and albums feature contemporary songs, Houston's roots are in gospel music. Her mother, Cissy Houston, was a gospel singing star and occasionally joins her daughter in concerts or on recordings. The younger Houston often credits her church upbringing for having a major influence on her professional career, as well as her personal life.

Not Just Gospel

The influence of Christianity on "urban" or hip-hop music is not as well known, but it is a growing subculture among hip-hop musicians. Hip-hop artists take part in gospel music conventions, their shows draw increasing numbers of young people, and magazines, and Web sites abound for fans.

Among prominent Christian hip-hop artists are dc Talk, Gospel Gangstaz, Mr. Del, New Breed, and Ill Harmonics. The wider "urban" sound, including R&B, dance, techno, and more, also can be heard performed with a Christian theme.

Islam's affect on African Americans also has a small impact on the music scene. Native Deen is one of several rap groups that identifies closely with traditional Islam. Three Muslim brothers comprise Native Deen, and follow their Islamic faith by not performing at bars or discos.

WE DEMAND
AN END
POLICE BRUTALITY
NOW!
WE DEMAND
DECENT HOUSING
NOW!
WE MARCH FOR
JOBS
FOR ALL
NOW!
WE DEMAND
EQUAL RIGHTS
NOW!
WE DEMAND
VOTING
FIRST BAPTIST CHURCH
DEANWOOD
PEOPLE ARE GAGGED and CHAINED—
THEY CANNOT VOTE
UAW SAYS:
END
SEGREGATED
RULES
IN
PUBLIC
SCHOOLS
UAW SAYS:
BEFORE
WE'LL BE
A SLAVE,

4

African America: Faith and Society

EARLY IN THE 20TH CENTURY, EDUCATOR AND CIVIL RIGHTS LEADER W.E.B. DuBois made the prophetic statement that "The problem of the 20th century is the problem of the color line." DuBois might well have offered that assessment about each of the preceding centuries in U.S. history. Despite notable progress on many fronts, the 21st century finds DuBois' assessment still relevant. Matters such as affirmative action, racial profiling, and employment discrimination still concern us all. One way to assess the impact of African American religion on social issues is to examine how it has addressed the racial issues so key to the nation and to African Americans.

The black church has done this in several ways. One approach has been to press the nation's political and social systems to operate in an equal and fair manner. Another approach has been to meet directly the needs and challenges that systemic inequality has created. A third has been to offer spiritual nurture to black people so they could have both the strength to endure the harsh realities they live with and the will to work to change those realities. A fourth approach has been to provide one form or another of withdrawal from negative circumstances.

Regardless of the approach, clergy and religiously active lay people have always been involved. The clergy are among the most highly respected leaders in the African-American community. They are spokespersons for God and for the Christian church, or else for the Islamic faith.

In earlier times, in a nation that openly called itself a "Christian nation," this gave even more weight to the status of the clergy. And because African-Americans believed that God bestowed freedom and human dignity, it was natural for clergy to go into action, and the divine will to be invoked, when freedom and dignity were denied. Clergy came to be classed as "Race men"[in a time when clergy were only male], a commonly used term that was used for those who were expected to champion the positive interests of black people.

Challenging the Systems

PRECEDING PAGE
Inspired to call for change
African-American religious leaders, such as Dr. Martin Luther King, Jr., third from left in the front row in this 1963 photograph, were among the earliest and most important leaders of the civil rights movement.

Among the earliest open, public challenges to discrimination in the United States was the creation of the independent black churches. The presence of these congregations and denominations was a statement to the larger church that it had not lived up to its gospel responsibility to be the inclusive family of God. In a similar line of thought, black clergy and laity called upon the governing bodies of the nation to live up to their responsibility to put into practice the principles set forth in the Declaration of Independence, the Constitution, and other statements growing out of the American Revolution. These documents claimed to be based on an understanding of God and human history that was the same as African-American religion held. It seemed to blacks that there was a common ground they could appeal to that would, with proper argument, bring results.

With this thinking, Rev. Absalom Jones (see chapter 1), representing the free blacks of Philadelphia, sent a petition to Congress in 1800 that caused quite a stir in that body. The petitioners wrote, ". . . the solemn compact, the Constitution, was violated by the trade of kidnapping . . . ." The petitioners urged Congress that the slave trade be ended and the degrading and inhumane situation of slavery itself be addressed. Petitioning became a common form of direct action used to fight for racial justice.

Another form used by blacks across the nation was the convention movement. Beginning in 1830, blacks elected regional delegates to annual national and state meetings called to organize and strategize around how to deal with the crucial issues facing the black community. At these conventions, as they were known, it was common for clergy to be well-represented among the delegates and to be in leadership positions. For instance, the very first National Negro Convention, held in Philadelphia in 1830, elected Bishop Richard Allen as its president. One of the secretaries of the New York State Convention of Negroes, in 1840, was the Rev. Henry Highland Garnett (1815–1882), who in 1865 became the first black person to address the U.S. House of Representatives. Reverend John J. Moore (1814–1893) was active in the California Negro Conventions, which began in 1855.

The speeches and resolutions that came from these meetings often carried a religious tone. For example, the State Convention of Ohio Negroes, 1849, spoke of the struggle of oppressed peoples around the globe for "that liberty which God has benignly given to all his creatures, and which will be wrested from them only by vampire despots."

Another avenue for challenging discrimination was journalism. The first newspaper to be published by African Americans, *Freedom's Journal*, began its weekly run in 1827. Its owner was John B. Russwurm, and its editor the Rev. Samuel Cornish. As the paper's name implied, it was dedicated to the liberation and uplift of black people. In 1837, Cornish and Phillip A. Bell founded the *Colored American*, with the Rev. Charles B. Ray as assistant editor. In California in the late 1850s, the Rev. John J. Moore founded the *Lunar Visitor*, a news journal that was adopted as the official organ of the State Convention of the Colored Citizens of the State of California. Many other publications committed to the rights and interests of African Americans have since been published with the help of clergy or churches, or have incorporated religious news in support of the publication's purposes.

African-American clergy, laity, and their churches participated in the Underground Railroad helping fugitive slaves to freedom, or serving on committees that helped guard free blacks from unlawful enslavement. Many clergy and laity were traveling abolitionist lecturers. In the early 20th century, blacks and their white supporters organized the National Association for the Advancement of Colored People (NAACP) and the Urban League, and black clergy were part of the founding groups. The Civil Rights movement, driven by such national groups as the Southern Christian Leadership Conference and local groups such as the Alamo Black Clergy (in Oakland/Berkeley, California) or Seattle's Black Clergy United for Action—all had clergy or

STRONG WORDS

The 1849 Ohio convention's "Declaration of Sentiments" included these words:

To sternly resist, by all the means which the God of Nations has placed in our power, every form of oppression or proscription attempted to be imposed upon us, in consequence of our condition or color.

To respect and love that as the religion of Jesus Christ . . . is not excitement merely, but that which loves God, loves humanity, and thereby preaches deliverance to the captives . . . .

strong laypersons in their leadership and churches in their support base.

In the opening years of the 21st century, individual clergy and laity, ministerial alliances, and national organizations such as PUSH (People United to Serve Humanity), headed by the Rev. Jesse L. Jackson, Sr. (b.1941; see page 109), continue to press the governmental and economic and legal systems of the country to operate with fairness and equity in relation to African Americans.

UNDERGROUND RAILROAD

The Underground Railroad was the name given to a series of escape routes, safe houses, and sympathetic men and women who cooperated, at risk, in secretly transporting slaves to freedom. The Underground Railroad was always helped by people involved in many different Christian religions.

Today the brave sacrifices of many of those people are memorialized through museums and educational exhibits. Another way to remember is through re-enactments like that of Joan Southgate, a 73-year-old grandmother of seven, who, in the spring of 2002, walked 359 miles from southern Ohio to northern Ohio, to honor the journey her ancestors made—a journey that ultimately put them in Canada and freedom. You can learn more about Southgate's walk at www.in-theirpath.com.

Addressing the Needs and Challenges

While some African Americans worked on getting the systems of society to function fairly, others put their energies into aiding black communities directly.

The Free African Society. Modern black-owned insurance companies and other financial service businesses can trace their heritage to the 18th-century Free African Society. The idea for this pioneering organization came from Absalom Jones and Richard Allen, also pioneers in the black church movement. Jones and Allen were concerned about the social and religious conditions of black Philadelphians and wanted to do something concrete to help. They first had in mind to form a religious organization, but the response among blacks was mixed. So they came up with an idea for a group that would meet monthly, each member contributing a set amount each time which would be used to help members who came into financial need through illness, job loss, or other misfortunes. There was to be no specific religious agenda for the organization, but members were expected to lead respectable, moral lives.

Officially established in May of 1787, the Free African Society was the first mutual aid society among African Americans. Soon similar groups were started in other cities. Over the years, some of them, such as the Free African Society, decided to become church congregations. In other cases, church congregations established mutual aid societies as part of their ministries. Some of these mutual aid societies developed into insurance and banking institutions.

Insurgency, Insurrection, Revolt. Sojourner Truth (1797?–1883) was a powerful, eloquent speaker. Though a Christian evangelist, she was renowned for her oratorical prowess on behalf of the abolition of slav-

Holy leadership
Three ministers (left to right): Joseph Lowery, Ralph Abernathy, and Andrew Young were among the leaders of the Southern Christian Leadership Conference, a civil rights organization with strong roots in African-American churches.

ery and the rights of women. The esteem and admiration in which she was held was matched in intensity by the fear and chagrin set off by a sister in the struggle, an abolitionist of a slightly different sort, Harriet Tubman (c.1821–1913.) Born in slavery in Maryland, Tubman and two brothers eventually escaped. But she went back to the region of her enslavement many times, to spirit other slaves away to freedom on the Underground Railroad that had rescued her. This railroad "conductor," this "Moses of her people," as she came to be known, made some 19 trips into the South, safely delivering as many as 300 from slavery to freedom. Tubman claimed that she had never lost a passenger from her "train." The story has it that Tubman carried a pistol and that anyone losing their nerve and attempting to turn back mid-journey was "persuaded" by her to stay the course. She was such a thorn in the side to the South that a large bounty was placed on her head.

Tubman helped white abolitionist John Brown plan his famous raid on Harper's Ferry in 1859, in which he and several followers seized the United States Armory and Arsenal at Harper's Ferry, Virginia. Brown was captured in the raid, and was later executed by the

SOJOURNER TRUTH

Abolitionist and women's rights advocate Sojourner Truth was born Isabella Baumfree in the late 18th century as a slave, and remained so for about 30 years. In 1827, she was granted her freedom through the New York Gradual Abolition Act and then worked as a maid.

When she was in her 40s, she felt called by God to travel and preach about Him. Another word for a traveler is a "sojurner," and she believed she was preaching the truth, so she gave herself a new name.

Her powerful preaching was focused mostly on evangelizing, but she spoke forcefully and often about women's rights and about an end to slavery. In all her arguments, she used scripture to back up her claims and points of view. She worked with mostly-white social reform groups, and traveled widely. In 1864, she became one of the first African-American women to visit a president when she met with Abraham Lincoln.

U.S. government for his actions. Only an illness that confined Tubman to bed prevented her from taking part in the raid. During the Civil War, which soon followed, she worked with the Union Army as a spy, a scout, and a nurse. She never shrank from placing herself in harm's way on behalf of the cause of freedom, believing that the dreams and omens by which she directed her courageous actions were supplied by God. Tubman and Sojourner Truth were members of the African Methodist Episcopal Zion Church.

After the war, Tubman devoted herself to securing educational and material support for freed people. On land she purchased adjacent to her home in Auburn, New York, she established a facility for the care of elderly and needy blacks, which was later named in her honor the Harriet Tubman Home for Indigent and Aged Negroes.

The 12 Knights. If Sojourner Truth intended to abolish slavery through verbal argument, and Harriet Tubman sought to undermine it and free some of its victims, others had in mind to assault it directly and force its elimination. From the onset of slavery in 1619 until its legal end with the Emancipation Proclamation of 1863, there were more than 200 reported slave revolts. Of course, none of them succeeded, but they prove false the claim of slaveholders that their black "property" were contented with their lot, except when disturbed by "outside agitators" from the North.

The most well-known of the many attempted revolts were those of Gabriel Proesser in Virginia, Denmark Vesey in South Carolina, and Nat Turner (see page 30) in Virginia. But a campaign on a larger scale than perhaps any other appears to have been efficiently planned, armed, and ready to roll out, averted only by signs that the nation, itself, was about to go to battle over slavery.

In 1846, in St. Louis, Missouri, African Methodist Episcopal minister Rev. Moses Dickson (1824–1902) and 11 other persons formed themselves into a secret organization called the 12 Knights of Tabor. The name Tabor was chosen because it was the Biblical location where a relatively small Israelite army was victorious over an enemy force of overwhelming numbers. The Knights' agenda was direct military action to confront U.S. slavery. For the next 10 years, while working with the Underground Railroad, the Knights organized some 47,000 men into an army to fight for black freedom.

With financial backing from sympathizers in the United States and England, the troops were disciplined and well-armed. They operated under a pledge of strictest secrecy, knowing how similar efforts, such as Turner's, had been betrayed and crushed. And they felt a strong assurance about what they were doing, certain that they were "instruments in God's hands." In letters cited in Herbert Aptheker's

A leader for freedom
Harriet Tubman's bravery in the face of threats to her life remains an inspiration. She was one of hundreds who risked their lives to bring slaves to freedom, and she remains a symbol of that important work.

1979 collection *A Documentary History of the Negro People in the United States*, they are quoted as saying, "God was on the side of justice" and would give them victory as "God was with Israel, and gave the victory to the bondsmen, though they were opposed by twenty times their number." These ideas were like those of Turner, a Baptist preacher, who believed that he and his movement were operating under divine purposes and by divine signs.

In July of 1857, the troops were told to be ready to move on command. They would move out from their various locations, fighting to the death along the way, and meeting up in Atlanta. They would decide next steps from there, depending on how events were going.

The command was about to be given, but the leaders of the organization sensed that the conflict between North and South was coming to a head and that God was about to move through these two camps to resolve the issue of slavery. That proved to be the case when the Civil War began.

Women's Clubs. "Lifting As We Climb" was the motto of the National Association of Colored Women (NACW), formed in 1896 by the merger of the National Federation of Afro-American Women and the National

Help from the Faithful

African-American leaders were not the only ones pushing for an end to slavery. White Christian denominations such as the Quakers were also clamoring for an end to the practice, based on their beliefs. In 1783, for example, a Philadelphia meeting of several hundred Quakers sent a petition to Congress. Here is an excerpt:

> *We have long beheld with sorrow the complicated evils produced by an unrighteous commerce which subjects many thousands of the human species to the deplorable State of Slavery. . . . We therefore earnestly solicit your Christian interposition to discourage and prevent so obvious an Evil, in such manner as under the influence of Divine Wisdom you shall see meet.*

In 1833, William Lloyd Garrison (1805–1879) formed the American Anti-Slavery Association as a means to rally wider support for abolition. Though they had little success in convincing many other white preachers to share their cause, the group helped the anti-slavery forces get more organized and gain more attention as the Civil War neared.

League of Colored Women. These were umbrella organizations for the growing series of women's clubs that were forming across the United States as channels for women to do important service in their communities. They were not religious organizations, as such, but they were made up of active laywomen who saw their service as an expression of their religious faith. For instance, in describing the work of the clubs, Mary Church Terrell, the first NACW president, wrote in the article "Club Work of Colored Women," quoted in the 1972 book *The Afro-Americans: Selected Documents*, "Homes, more homes, better homes, purer homes, is the text upon which our sermons have been and will be preached." Terrell was saying that the clubs were acting out their beliefs ("sermons") in working for a better life for African Americans.

With such formidable women among the organizers of the NACW as Harriet Tubman and anti-lynching crusader Ida B. Wells Barnett, one can imagine the energy and effectiveness of the Association and its clubs. The Phillis Wheatley Club of New Orleans established a sanitarium and training school for nurses; club women in Tennessee worked for the repeal of Jim Crow laws; the national office raised money for schools, job training, senior housing, and child care, among its many projects. Most states eventually had a branch of the NACW. It remains active into the 21st century.

Urban Social Ministry. After Emancipation, the church was the first line of resource for helping the 3.5 million newly-freed blacks make the transition into the rights and responsibilities of freedom. As African Americans shifted their primary residential location from rural to urban areas, the church faced new challenges in its role as the keeper of the minds, souls, and bodies of black people. It had always functioned in multiple capacities, filling in for all those places of material and social benefit that prejudice prevented blacks from entering. The issues and strains of city life made the church's role even more complex and crucial. It responded on many fronts.

The movement of blacks into the cities of the South and, even more so, the North was the largest internal migration the nation had ever experienced. Black churches received these migrants and helped them in their adjustment to city life. They helped with transportation, finding housing, and finding places to worship.

Several congregations already had social service programs, such as employment and housing bureaus. These now were expanded and made available to the migrants. For instance, Chicago's Olivet Baptist Church added a kindergarten; a day nursery; a health bureau and free clinic; classes in nutrition and home health care, staffed by Red Cross nurses; a Temperance Society (WCTU); Boy Scouts; a Housing and Rooming Directorate; a Working Girls' Home; a Flat Owning Association; a branch of the Chicago Public Library; and a regular screening of movies, offered for education and entertainment. The church employed a staff of 16 to operate and coordinate these and other religious and social programs. And the church purchased a bus to transport youth and the aged back and forth. Quinn Chapel AME had a kindergarten, a reading room and library, an employment service, and a savings bank. Quinn and Olivet had both served as stations on the Underground Railroad during slavery.

In 1911, Wayman AME solicited in the *Chicago Defender* for men to help form an intergenerational organization "for the betterment of social, moral, religious, and political conditions of the colored men."

In 1900, AME Rev. Reverdy Ransom (1906–1957) founded the Institutional Church and Social Settlement. Under Ransom and his successor, Archibald J. Carey, Sr. (see page T81), Institutional operated a host of programs, including a day nursery, a kindergarten, a mother's club, an employment bureau, a print shop, a gym, and classes in cooking, sewing, and music. Articles in the *Chicago Daily News* for December, 1916, reported that Institutional AME, Walters AME Zion, and many other black churches offered social programs and support services that kept them open 24 hours a day. And nearly all of them were said to have active employment agencies. In 1916, Pilgrim Baptist had a cooperative buying club. Beyond the church, Evangelist Amanda Berry Smith (1837–1915) ran her Industrial School for Girls.

Not all or even most black congregations had this variety of ministries. Not all had the type of leadership or the resources to do so. Some focused on being a supportive community and a safe space for migrants to be encouraged and cared for spiritually and psychologically, while gradually making their way into urban culture. Both these church models stood well within the traditions of black church ministry.

Helping Out Today

The model of African-American churches helping in the community continues. For instance, on a national level today, the AME Church works with the Fannie Mae government home loan program to match recipients to loan programs and help members and others with the paperwork. Examples on a local level include Allen Temple AME, Cincinnati, Ohio, which co-sponsors an adult literacy program; operates a counseling service, a legal clinic, and a Minority Health Project; conducts discussion sessions on family issues such as communication, elder care, and single parenting. Allen Temple Baptist, Oakland, California, offers, among its many ministries, a tutoring program, health screening and education, senior citizens housing, employment assistance, a credit union, direct economic assistance, an athletics and recreation program, and a counseling ministry.

Trinity UCC of Chicago sponsors a major annual educational conference on AIDS, with practical workshops on AIDS ministry. It is commonplace for black congregations, large and small, to offer weekly meal service for the homeless. Some add clothing banks and personal counseling. The Fisher AME Zion Church, of Evanston, Illinois, assists the homeless and ex-offenders with employment, housing, and other support. In many ways, large and small, churches and their members take the lessons they learn in worship into the world around them.

Islam and the African-American Spirit

Islam has received a mixed reception among African Americans. On the one hand, Islam's followers have gained respect and admiration because of their insistent practice of their religion. Enslaved Muslims were known to defy both their owner's expectations as well as the typical lifestyles of other enslaved Africans in order to follow the disciplines and requirements of their faith. As such, they set a model for bold self-assertion in the face of dominating power structures.

Post-slavery Islam often has continued and even actively advanced this kind of counter-cultural, defiant posture. Moorish Scientists, a group formed in 1913 by Noble Drew Ali, called African Americans to identify themselves as Moors, an ancient term for Muslims from Africa, and to reject all imposed or even self-adopted racial labels, seeing these as either demeaning or putting blacks into a socially stigmatized "box."

Every little bit helps
In Los Angeles, Project Islamic Hope, directed by Najee Ali, seated, runs several community service programs, including a women's homeless center, while also working for social and legal reforms.

The Nation of Islam called upon blacks to reject Christianity, the "white man's religion," and to claim Islam, said to be the religion of their own heritage, from their own homeland. The Nation's teachings condemned white racism and even portrayed whites as the result of a creation process that had taken an evil turn. Racial discrimination and social/economic oppression in the United States were sharply criticized, and blacks were encouraged to defend themselves against assaults of any kind.

Further, Nation of Islam followers were to empower themselves and thus remove themselves from dependency on whites by building up an alternative structure of community institutions and economic enterprises. Blacks were even to seek from the government as many as five states for exclusive black habitation. At the same time, black worth and integrity were strongly affirmed; one was to take pride in oneself and the heritage of one's people. That pride, in turn, was to be embodied in one's life, so rules and guidelines were set forth for how to live respectable, socially productive, disciplined, law-abiding lives.

The combination of fearless defiance of whites and strong affirmation of the present and historical integrity of black people had appeal for blacks, generally, who had suffered under centuries of white oppression and personal denigration. It was especially attractive for those segments of the black community on the margins of American society, with little self-esteem or hope for social advancement. Thus, while the various Islamic movements gained limited black membership compared to the black Christian churches, they gained considerably wider sympathy and moral support. Malcolm X (see page 40) was and continues to be a highly celebrated figure in the black community. Another fiery Muslim orator and leader, Minister Louis Farrakhan, also enjoys wide appeal, though some of his alleged anti-Semitic and anti-white statements have made him a very controversial figure. Building on the deep concern many blacks hold about the social challenges faced by African-American males, Farrakhan was a key figure in organizing the 1995 Million Man March (see page 83); he continues to command large audiences for public addresses.

A Shift and Further Controversy

The African-American Islamic community underwent a significant shift in 1975. Following the death of Nation of Islam leader Elijah Muhammad (see page 39), his son, Warith Deen Muhammad (b. 1933; see page 105), led a portion of the Nation's members to form the the American Muslim Mission. Adhering to traditional Muslim piety and practices, the group counts more than 2 million members, primarily African Americans. Blacks now make up the largest single ethnic group within American Islam.

On the other hand, while black Christians can be counted among those who have privately or openly supported the social advocacy thrust of Islam, there have also been some causes for tension, even contention with this faith. Islam in general represents a basically different faith than Christianity, even though both hold the Old Testament to be an authoritative religious text. And the Nation of Islam, as has been said, even attacked Christianity as a religion that supports slavery and black oppression. For many African-American Christians, Islam represents a cultural tradition that is foreign to their world and also a faith that is in opposition to the faith they believe was the foundation of black survival. Islam, as with other religions, is seen by some black Christian groups as, at best, a field for evangelism and, at worst, an opponent in the struggle for spirituality in America.

AMERICA2

5

Politics: On the Outside Looking in

UNTIL THE LATE 19TH CENTURY, THE LAWS AND CUSTOMS OF MOST colonies and later most states prohibited African Americans from any direct participation in the nation's political processes. They were not allowed to vote, nor were they eligible to hold public office. Therefore, any effect blacks were to have on politics had to come by persuading those who held such rights that they should honor African-American needs and interests.

To accomplish this, blacks used three basic arguments. First, they argued that to grant full citizens' rights to them was called for by the noble principles on which the nation was founded—principles voiced in the speeches justifying the Revolution, in the Declaration of Independence, and in the United States Constitution. In 1774, enslaved blacks in Massachusetts petitioned the state legislature for their freedom, saying, "We have in common with all other men a natural right to our freedoms." In 1780, seven blacks protested to the Massachusetts state legislature that blacks were being heavily taxed while denied the right to vote. This "taxation without representation" was, they said, "contrary to the invariable custom and practice of the country." They said that this was truly unjust since a higher percentage of the black population volunteered to serve in the Revolutionary army than any other group.

It was in this same spirit of calling the nation to live up to its own principles and do justice to blacks that AME Zion minister Rev. John J. Moore (1814–1893) challenged white Californians to "go forward to the Declaration of Independence." (This was found in Moore's writings in San Francisco's *Elevator* newspaper.)

Another argument blacks used in seeking rights and fair treatment was that their conduct showed they deserved it. As much as any other segment of the population, they obeyed the laws, kept decent homes, held regular employment, and minded their own business. When accusations were made that blacks were prone to crime or that they were a drain on government resources, they produced public records that showed blacks consistently were represented in lower numbers and lower proportions among crime statistics and among public assistance recipients than whites.

PRECEDING PAGE
Nearly at the top
By 2000, when Jesse Jackson spoke at the Democratic National Convention, African Americans had made tremendous progress in their involvement in American politics—a path often led by religious leaders.

Third, blacks argued that justice, fairness, and freedom from oppression were the will of God for all people and that the United States, as a self-professed Christian nation, should honor God's will. For instance, in 1797, four emancipated blacks in Philadelphia who were wrongfully being re-enslaved petitioned Congress for help, on the grounds that the members of Congress "under God, the sovereign Ruler of the Universe, are entrusted with the distribution of justice."

In stronger language, New York writer Robert Alexander Young published a pamphlet in 1829 (reprinted in *Aptheker*) in which he asserted that, "God decrees to [the] slave his rights as a man. Therefore, slaveholders should take heed that. . . the decree hath already passed the judgment seat of an undeviating God, wherein he hath said, 'surely hath the cries of the black, a most persecuted people, ascended to my throne and craved my mercy.'" God was going to bring great affliction on slaveholders if slavery continued, said Young.

In the same year, Bostonian David Walker's pamphlet, *Walker's Appeal*, boldly called on blacks to seize their freedom by force when the right moment arrived, with the assurance that "Jesus Christ the King of Heaven and of earth who is the God of justice and armies, will surely go before you." Like Young, Walker had a warning for the nation if it did not undo the brutal system of slavery: "Americans of the United States, though they may for a little while escape, God will yet weigh them in a balance . . . he will give them wretchedness to their very heart's content."

A contemporary of Young and Walker, Phillip Alexander Bell (1807–1889), a pioneer black journalist, published an editorial in the *Elevator*, April 28, 1865, asserting that human rights and civil freedoms were gifts to all from God. Therefore humans could not take them away. It was almost as though he saw in national events the fulfillment of Young's and Walker's prophecies, for Bell claimed that the Civil War was a case of God using the terrible force of war to scourge the nation for its oppression and to restore to blacks their right to freedom.

One hundred years later, echoes of the argument of justice and freedom for blacks being part of God's vision for the world could still be heard. In his famous "I Have a Dream" speech, made before the crowd at the historic 1963 march on Washington, Rev. Dr. Martin Luther King, Jr., compared America's unfulfilled Constitutional promise of inalienable rights for all to the fulfillment of the Biblical promise of God that "every valley shall be exalted, every mountain and hill made low, the crooked places made straight and the rough places plain, and the glory of God shall be revealed, all flesh shall see it together." (Isaiah 40:4-5) For while King's dream was, in his words, "deeply rooted in the American dream," he understood that dream, itself, to be rooted in the Judeo-Christian tradition. At the center of this tradition was the God who was revealed in Scripture as one who intervened in history to uphold human liberation and who intended for humans to live in communities characterized by love and justice.

POWERFUL WORDS

In 1779, a group of slaves in Connecticut presented "The Petition of the Negroes in the Towns of Stratford and Fairfield in the County of Fairfield Who are held in a State of Slavery." In it, they sought release from bondage on the grounds that

Reason & Revelation join to declare, that we are the Creatures of that God, who made of one Blood, and Kindred, all the Nations of the Earth . . . . [W]e are Convinced of our Right (by the Laws of Nature and by the whole Tenor of the Christian Religion, so far as we have been taught) to be free.

In, but Out

Perhaps the most basic way that African-American religion has affected political processes has been by assuring blacks that by "Reason & Revelation," they had a right to be in the process, that it was God's will for them to be so. This provided the encouragement and the justification to challenge their exclusion, to be persistent in pressing local and national lawmakers to "do the right thing" and include them, even when the prospects seemed dim.

At the same time, the independent black congregations and denominational bodies became training grounds for political participation. In church, one could vote on church issues, elect officers, and lobby for programs and policies according to one's best judgment. In church, clergy and lay community leaders could share information about issues of concern so that through personal contacts with whites or through organized efforts, they could influence the outcome of public issues. And when organization was the route taken, strategies were often debated and planned in church buildings and with clergy participation. What issues will we focus on? What influential white person will help us? Shall we petition or boycott? What will the costs be and how shall finances be raised? Without an actual vote and without public officials who were responsible by election to represent them, blacks had to use these indirect means to be in the process while they were outside the power structure.

KEY RELIGIOUS GROUPS

Here are some examples of national church-based organizations whose use their ministry to try to affect social change through a variety of means.

Congress of National Black Churches

Darkstar Community Outreach Center

People United to Serve Humanity

Quitman County (Mississippi) Development Organization

Southern Christian Leadership Conference

Union of Black Episcopalians

Agitating to Stay and Be Free

Two of the more important and long-running forms of indirect political action were participation in the anti-colonization movement and lecturing in the abolition movement.

From the earliest colonial days there were tensions concerning the presence of Africans in the country. As colonial settlement moved forward and the labor needs for developing the settlements became clearer, there were those who were firm in their belief that slavery was necessary for the success of the enterprise. This position was especially strong in the Middle and Southern colonies, where agriculture came to dominate the economy. Others, however, saw deep problems in maintaining a growing population of people who were in forced bondage—a bondage that raised religious and moral questions, and whose racial character made it unlikely that they could ever merge into the larger population. How are they to be contained? What is to be their social and civil status? The status of their children? Are they full humans, or property, or both? What does all this mean and how are they to fit into our society?

Thomas Jefferson was one who wondered about these issues. He was a Founding Father and third U.S. president, an author of the vision of what the new nation would be, and he was a major slaveholder. He had serious concerns, even fears, about a future United States that included the institution of slavery. He, like others, faced the question of what to do with the hundreds of thousands of Africans that were already in the country and growing in numbers.

One solution that drew serious attention was to transport free blacks and emancipated slaves to some other, faraway place. The

American Colonization Society (ACS) was founded in 1817 to accomplish this purpose. Its membership included some of the nation's very wealthy and prominent citizens, including slave owners and slavery supporters. The country of Liberia, with its capital city of Monrovia named after U.S. president James Monroe, was established as the place where the emancipated were to be colonized.

While this project might have seemed to be a positive answer to the slavery dilemma, blacks almost universally saw a sinister motive in it. Evidence suggested that the real goal was to drain off the free black population so that they would no longer be role models for the enslaved or sources of agitation for their liberation. So while there were some blacks who saw the program of the ACS as an opportunity

Words of Freedom

Here are excerpts of the Constitutional amendments that helped free slaves and expand the right to vote.

Amendment XIII (1865)
Neither slavery nor involuntary servitude, except as a punishment for crime whereof the party shall have been duly convicted, shall exist within the United States, or any place subject to their jurisdiction.

Amendment XIV (1868)
No state shall make or enforce any law which shall abridge the privileges or immunities of citizens of the United States; nor shall any state deprive any person of life, liberty, or property, without due process of law; nor deny to any person within its jurisdiction the equal protection of the laws.

Amendment XV (1870)
The right of citizens of the United States to vote shall not be denied or abridged by the United States or by any state on account of race, color, or previous condition of servitude.

to escape U.S. oppression, black clergy and laity generally criticized the ACS and opposed its operation. For instance, each of the pre-Civil War meetings of the Annual National Negro Convention, and several of the state-level conventions, specifically addressed and condemned the ACS as pursuing a wrong-headed program which served only to solidify slavery in the United States.

Aside from its cooperation with supporters of slavery, colonization felt to many blacks like being uprooted from what had become their home. It was home in a land that held hope and promise of greatness, if the evil blot of slavery could be eliminated. Therefore, blacks were actively involved in the campaign for the abolition of slavery. We have already seen in chapter 4 that strong laywomen Harriet Tubman and Sojourner Truth were regular abolitionist lecturers, as was layman Frederick Douglass (1818–1895). Future bishop of the AME Church Daniel Payne (1811–1893) spoke regularly to abolitionist gatherings. Presbyterian minister Henry Highland Garnet (1815–1882) was an energetic abolitionist and co-founder of the American and Foreign Anti-Slavery Society. The list is long of clergy and laypersons who devoted years to preaching, speaking, and writing about abolishing slavery.

The Door Swings Open—Sort of

The Civil War brought the emancipation of all slaves in the states in rebellion. The 13th Amendment to the Constitution abolished slavery in all states and territories. The 14th and 15th Amendments completed the legal admission of African-Americans to the rights and prerogatives of citizenship, including the right to vote and hold office. (Only males of any race could vote at this time.)

Blacks moved with satisfaction and also thoughtfulness to take advantage of their new freedoms. They considered the issues, evaluated candidates for office, and fielded candidates of their own. They elected persons to office on the local, state, and national levels.

Of course, this did not happen without a challenge. Whites, especially in the South, resisted the movement of blacks into decision-making roles. And so, for instance, the Rev. Henry McNeal Turner (1834–1915) was elected to the Georgia State Senate in 1868, but in September of that year Georgia ejected all of its black legislators. In some places, voting officials refused to allow blacks to register. On into the 20th century, access to voting remained a prime civil rights issue.

Sometimes the roadblocks placed before blacks reached the point of the ridiculous, as when to qualify to vote they were required to recite the Constitution backwards or to state how many bubbles there were in a bar of soap!

Though ridiculous, this matter could also be deadly. Claiming one's civil rights, or educating people about their rights and leading them in the exercise of those rights, has been the occasion for the dismissal from jobs, the burning of property, and the savage murder of untold numbers of men and women over the years.

But the door was not to be closed again. Step by step black religious people moved more fully into political participation.

A Pair of Preacher-Politicians

Not all, and perhaps not most, church leaders were directly involved in the political arena. But there are outstanding examples of the many who were. In Chicago, the Rev. Archibald Carey, Jr., (1908–1981) who

A place at the table
Prominent Chicago-based preacher/politician Archibald Carey, Jr., is shown between Mamie Eisenhower and President Dwight D. Eisenhower at a White House event in 1953. Second from right is Branch Rickey, a baseball executive who signed Jackie Robinson, the first African-American major league baseball player.

Their man in Washington
A colorful man, a vibrant speaker, and one of New York's most prominent citizens for most of his life, the Rev. Adam Clayton Powell, Jr., was a minister, city councilman, and congressman.

was the pastor of Institutional, Bethel, Woodlawn, and Quinn Chapel AME Churches, became a formidable political force. He played a major role in the election of William Hale Thompson as alderman and later as mayor of Chicago (1915). Carey, himself, was an alderman of the City Council from 1947-55. Local and national politicians spoke from his pulpits. He could turn out the black voters of Chicago in large numbers behind campaigns against vice and racial discrimination. He won their support for candidates for office that he felt would best advance black interests. His value as a public figure was recognized on the national level, as well, where he served, among other positions, as the first black to chair a White House committee, the President's Committee on Government Employment Policy. Carey biographer Joseph Logsdon wrote in his 1961 doctoral thesis "Rev. Archibald Carey and the Negro in Chicago Politics," "Political decisions by Archibald Carey were made primarily on the basis of what politicians offered his race. Politics for him was an extension of the racial protests and demands that he carried on throughout his life."

In New York, the Rev. Adam Clayton Powell, Jr., (1908–1972) succeeded his father as pastor of the Abyssinian Baptist Church in Harlem, then the largest black congregation in the nation. Following in his father's path of community involvement, he instituted many new social service programs through the church and was an active leader of community movements for social justice, especially fair employment practices. In 1941, he was elected as the first black member of the New York City Council, and in 1944 the people of Harlem sent him as their representative to Congress. His style of leadership in that body was brash and audacious. He challenged race discrimination and white privilege in every aspect of his work. A very effective congressional leader, Powell receives major credit for integrating the military and for orchestrating the passage of the 1961 Minimum Wage Bill, the Manpower Development and Training Act, the Anti-Poverty Bill, and the Vocational Education Act. Powell served in Congress for 25 years.

A Continuing Tradition

From the time of Carey and Powell up to today, there are many examples of the continuing impact of African-American religion on the political arena. Persons such as Malcolm X and Martin Luther King, Jr. planted seeds for a major shift in the nation's thinking about matters that went beyond race. They pointed to the inconsistency between our national ideals and the inequitable, socially destructive functioning of our capitalistic system, our employment policies, our international political dealings, and our military campaigns. For instance, in his later years, King was an important critic of U.S. involvement in Vietnam.

Others have added their particular emphases, working for social and political change either through their churches and temples, through social organizations, or within the government, itself. Revs. William Gray (b. 1941), Walter Fauntroy (b.1933), and Floyd Flake (b.1945) are among the clergy who have served in Congress while actively pastoring local congregations. Rev. Andrew Young (b.1932) was a staff person in the Southern Christian Leadership Conference (SCLC), where he served under Martin Luther King and helped draft the Civil Rights Act of 1964 and the Voting Rights Act of 1965. He was elected to Congress from Georgia in 1972 and served until he was appointed by President Jimmy Carter to be ambassador to the United Nations in 1977. Later Young served two terms as mayor of Atlanta. Rev. Jesse L. Jackson, Sr., who also served with King, went on to found Operation PUSH (People United to Serve Humanity) and the Rainbow

The Million Man March

African-American Muslims have worked to have a voice in the political arena, too. On October 16, 1995, hundreds of thousands of African-American men gathered in Washington D.C. for a rally called by Nation of Islam leader Louis Farrakhan. The "Million Man March" was designed to raise awareness of the issues facing the African-American community.

Celebrities such as Stevie Wonder and politicians, including Rev. Jesse Jackson and members of Congress, attended and spoke to the massive crowd. Men came from around the country to be part of the event.

A man of many talents
Rev. Andrew Young (left), shown here with Dr. Martin Luther King, Jr., has served with distinction in civil rights posts, as a congressman from Georgia, as a United Nations ambassador, and as mayor of Atlanta.

Coalition. These organizations are dedicated to the advancement of African-Americans and also other disadvantaged peoples. Jackson competed for the Democratic nomination for president in 1984 and 1988, earning millions of votes and advancing farther than any other African American in that important contest.

A Final Note About the Vote

From the early days of black social and political activism, the right to vote, and thus to help determine legislation and leadership, has been a central concern. Once it was extended through the U.S. Constitution, it still had to be put into practice and defended on the local level, against much ongoing opposition. And so, much of black political impact has been in the area of seeking and using the vote—and not just for blacks alone. Black civil rights activists were also involved in the campaign for women's suffrage, and have worked to extend voting privileges to all excluded groups.

Once gaining the vote, black citizens have used it effectively. Though always a minority segment of the population, they have been a large enough voting bloc to determine the outcome of elections, especially close ones. This has been the source of another point of African-American religion's impact on political issues: Office seekers and campaigners for particular issues have made it a practice to befriend black clergy, in hopes that the clergy would influence the support of their congregations. Taking it more directly, at election time, campaigners make the Sunday morning rounds of black churches, requesting and typically being granted the chance to make their case to the congregations. Black voters traditionally have exercised savvy and thoughtfulness in the use of this important citizen's right.

An Election Mess

In November 2000, America voted for a new president, choosing between Vice President Al Gore and Texas Governor George W. Bush. In the closest race in more than 100 years, Bush won by the narrowest of margins. However, he didn't officially win until many weeks after the election when the Supreme Court ruled on the final tally in the state of Florida. Florida's voting system encountered dozens of problems in counting its crucial votes, and the delays had the country on edge for weeks.

The fight in Florida over voting was about the machines used to count the votes, but it was also about how some ballots were removed from the counting. To some, the choices about what ballots were removed was based on race, and black churches were among the most vocal critics of the seemingly endless vote-counting process.

In "Botched Ballots" (posted January 12, 2001, on abcnews.com), Dan Harris reported that pastors in Florida were taking to the pulpits to demand action on the voting crisis and to call attention to what they saw as racially unfair decisions. He quoted these two preachers.

"If our ancestors fought to get us the right to vote, then our vote ought to count," said Rev. Rudolf McKissic, Jr., of the Bethel Baptist Missionary Church in Jacksonville.

"Someone is trying to steal this election," Bishop Victor Curry told his congregation at the New Birth Baptist Church in Miami.

Rev. Jesse Jackson was also a vocal critic of the process and held rallies in Florida.

As has been the case throughout American history, in times of crisis, whether spiritual, economic, or political, many African Americans turned to their churches and ministers for answers and action.

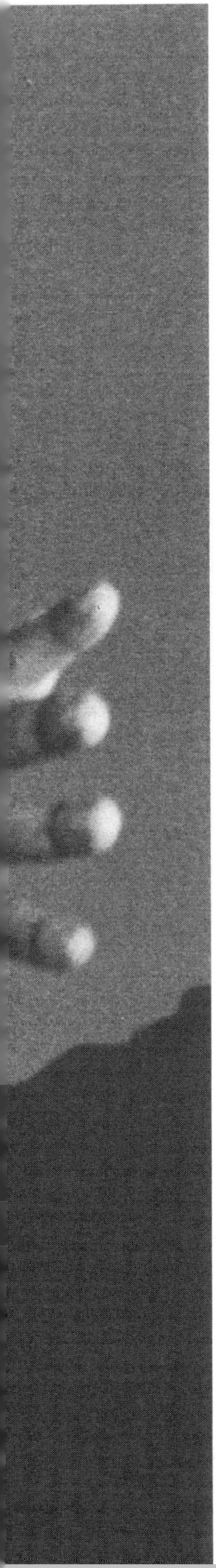

6

Important Leaders in Faith and More

OVER THE CENTURIES OF AFRICAN PRESENCE IN WHAT IS NOW THE United States, countless women and men have contributed significantly to the African-American religious experience. Some of them have been heralded and celebrated; some have passed without recognition, except in their local circles of acquaintance. All have been important. In earlier chapters, many of these people were highlighted. In this chapter we will sketch the lives of more people, some familiar and others less well-known, who represent aspects of the diversity of African-American religion.

Richard Allen (1760–1831)

Born into slavery in colonial Philadelphia, Richard Allen rose above the boundaries of his birth to become one of the new nation's most distinguished citizens. By 1767, Allen's family was sold to a Delaware farmer. In his teen years, Allen's farm was visited by one of the traveling preachers of the fledgling Methodist movement. He and his brother were converted to Christianity. They were strongly affected by their new faith and even led their owner to also embrace Christianity.

Allen and his brother were allowed to work for wages to accumulate money to purchase their freedom. Achieving that goal by the time the

Revolutionary War ended in 1781, Allen became a traveling Methodist preacher, going on evangelistic journeys with noted Methodist leaders Richard Whatcoat (1736–1806) and Francis Asbury (1745–1816).

An incident that occurred during Allen's travels with Asbury provided an early sign of the direction of the young preacher's personal convictions and his public leadership. It was the practice in those days for traveling preachers to take lodging in households on their preaching circuit. But racial attitudes of the time dictated that while blacks could preach to white audiences, even be a pastor to a white congregation, they were not to be permitted to interact socially on equal terms with whites. When on their preaching mission, Asbury was invited to sleep in a family's home but conceded to racial practice and informed Allen that he must sleep in the carriage. Allen declared this to be unacceptable Christian practice and discontinued any further joint missions of this type. In Allen, deeply-held Christian belief combined with deeply-held respect for the integrity of black people.

PRECEDING PAGE
Powerful preacher
Rev. Martin Luther King, Jr., brought the messages of peace, justice, and love from his faith into the social and political world–in the process becoming one of the world's most important civil rights leaders.

It is not surprising, then, that when Allen arrived in Philadelphia, he looked for a way to address the spiritual needs of black Philadelphians, who were not being served by the existing religious bodies. Though this did not work out initially, Allen, along with Absolom Jones and others, took the lead in drawing blacks in 1787 into an organization, the Free African Society, that provided moral, spiritual, and physical care for its members. Allen and Jones led black Philadelphians in a volunteer effort which put the volunteers' own lives in jeopardy to tend to city residents infected by the Yellow Fever epidemic of 1793. These same two had been at the center of a walkout of blacks from St. George Methodist Church in 1787 in response to discriminatory treatment (see page 26). Allen went on to organize an independent black Methodist congregation and was the first bishop to serve in the new African Methodist Episcopal denomination, incorporated in 1816.

Allen's leadership in the religious and social arenas of the African-American community was also expressed in many other ways, including his open letter to slaveholders urging them, on behalf of justice and under threat of Divine judgment, to abandon the practice of slavery. In fact, he became known and highly respected across the free black North—perhaps the first person to achieve national black leadership status. As such a leader, in 1830 he was elected president of the first Annual National Negro Conventions, a gathering called to consider and strategize the needs and concerns of blacks in the United States. Allen died six months later, in March, 1831, but his name is broadly recognized even today as a symbol of pious, courageous, effective advocacy for inclusive justice in the human family.

Dr. James W.C. Pennington (c.1808–1870)

In the 19th century, the title "Doctor" was not often associated with African-Americans. But one man fully earned it by a rich international career in ministry, though his humble beginnings did not seem to hold promise for such success.

James Pennington was born into slavery in Maryland in about 1808. He experienced all the harshness of the life of the enslaved, including the pain of separation when family members were sold apart. No longer willing to take it, he ran away to Pennsylvania at about age 21. Friendly Quakers gave him lodging and started him on the path to education—a path he traveled and led others on for the rest of his life. Perhaps in tribute to those who had taken him in, James adopted his first host's name, William, and added as his last name one that was associated with Quakers, Pennington.

A trip to the past
James Pennington played an important role in the Amistad *affair (see page 91). This photo shows a scene from the 1997 movie* Amistad *that retold this little-known episode in American history. Here the slaves from the ship are rowing in one of the ship's rowboats. Standing at the front of the boat is actor Djimon Hounsou, who played the revolt leader Joseph Cinque.*

Moving to Brooklyn, New York, in 1829, he pursued his education through night classes and private tutoring. Pennington apparently was a voracious learner, for within a few years after his escape from slavery he had taught himself to read and write and had become competent in English, German, Latin, and Greek. He valued education highly and wanted all African Americans to share in its benefits. In 1833 he found work as a teacher at a school in New Town, Long Island, the first of many times he accepted the role of educator.

Pennington also had a gift for public speaking. This served him well in his vocation of Christian ministry and its application to issues of social justice. In 1835 he pursued a calling into the ordained ministry, taking coursework in divinity and becoming active in church leadership. He was ordained in the Congregational Church. One of his early noteworthy services as a minister was to officiate at the wedding of distinguished abolitionist orator Frederick Douglass.

Pennington's gifts as an eloquent speaker and effective church leader were recognized widely. He pastored several congregations, and was twice elected as moderator of his local church association. He was a speaker at the first of the National Negro Conventions in 1831, and was a delegate to four more of these key gatherings. Internationally, Pennington represented the Connecticut Anti-Slavery Society at the 1843 World's Anti-Slavery Convention in London, where he also was the delegate of the American Peace Society to the World's General Peace Convention. Between that trip and a later one in 1849, sponsored by the Glasgow Female Anti-Slavery Society, he lectured and preached several times in England, Scotland, France, and Belgium.

Rev. Pennington was also an author. He compiled the first published history of African Americans, *The Textbook of the Origin and History (etc., etc) of the Colored People* (1841). In 1849, he published his autobiography, *The Fugitive Blacksmith; or, Events in the History of James W.C. Pennington*, which was widely read.

In addition, Pennington worked for racial and social justice, cofounding the New York Legal Rights Association, acting as president of the Union Missionary Society (which urged the boycott of slave-made goods), and writing for *Anglo-African* magazine. Late in his life, he was awarded the honorary doctor of divinity degree by the University of Heidelberg in Germany, the first African American to be so honored by a European institution.

Pennington and the Amistad Mutiny

In 1839, about 40 slaves being carried on the *Amistad*, a small ship sailing from Africa to Cuba, overcame their captors, killed the crew, and took over the vessel. They tried to sail back to Africa, but were taken by an American Navy ship. A great controversy erupted over what to do with the Africans. Cuba demanded their return, while American government officials wanted to try the escaped slaves for murder.

James Pennington and white abolitionist Lewis Tappan rallied behind the cause of the men on trial and organized a defense of the mutineers. The case went all the way to the U.S. Supreme Court, where former president John Quincy Adams argued for the Africans. They won their case and their freedom and returned to the African nation of Sierra Leone.

In 1997, Steven Spielberg made a movie about the case. The film, called *Amistad*, starred Anthony Hopkins as John Quincy Adams, Morgan Freeman as abolitionist Theodore Joadson, and Djimon Hounsou as the slave revolt leader Joseph Cinque.

Biddy Mason (1818–1891)

In August of 1818, a girl child given the name Bridget was born to enslaved parents on a Georgia plantation. At some point thereafter, her ownership was transferred to the Robert Smith family of Mississippi. With them, Bridget became a skilled herbalist and midwife (a person who assists women in childbirth).

In 1847, Smith, a Mormon, gathered his family, slaves, and other possessions and journeyed with a caravan of Mormons headed to the new Utah Territory to establish a Mormon community in the Salt Lake Basin. Bridget, now known as Biddy, was taken along on this westward trek. And trek it truly was, for Biddy walked the length of the overland journey, herding the sheep as the Smith family rode in the wagons. Smith's sojourn in Utah was short-lived. In 1851 he joined another Mormon settlement party, this time going to San Bernardino, in southern California. Once, again, Biddy walked along.

As fortune would have it, though, this trek turned out ultimately to be a long walk toward freedom. California had been admitted to the Union in 1850 as a free state. When Smith realized what this meant for his ownership of slaves, he prepared to move his family to the slavery-supporting state of Texas. But three African Americans whom Biddy had befriended, Charles Owens, Manuel Pepper, and Elizabeth Rowan, filed a lawsuit in the California courts seeking Biddy's freedom. In light of California's laws forbidding slavery and, thus, disallowing anyone to be forced from the state against their will, the court ruled in Biddy's favor; Smith forfeited his "property."

Somewhere along the line, Biddy had taken the surname Mason. She developed a reputation as an excellent midwife. And though she was unable to read or write, she began to accumulate wealth through real estate investments, eventually owning large tracts of land in what is now downtown Los Angeles. For just one of her many parcels of land she once turned down an offer of $200,000, deciding, instead, to leave that land to her family.

Biddy was a Christian and a generous supporter of charitable causes. She gave personal counsel and financial aide to the imprisoned, the homeless, the poor, and victims of natural disaster, regardless of race. She donated portions of her land holdings for the construction of schools, churches, and hospitals. It was in her home and with her encouragement that in 1872 Los Angeles' first African-American church, First African Methodist Episcopal, was organized. For a period of time she paid the taxes on the church property and also the minister's salary. First AME today is a significant Los Angeles institution, in part thanks to Biddy Mason's generosity.

The Emigration Triumvirate

As we saw in chapter 2, there has long been debate over what should be the place of African Americans in American society. Many whites came to feel that their place should be away from the United States. Interestingly, some African Americans also arrived at the conclusion that relocation was the best available solution for black well-being and progress. In 1829 some blacks in Cincinnati moved to a settlement near London, Ontario; a large group of black Californians in 1858 went to British Columbia. Over the course of the 19th century, several destination points were suggested to which some or all of the African-American population should emigrate.

The continent of Africa has always been a place of fascination and possibility for blacks in the United States. It was acknowledged as the homeland, even if there were those who could not, or did not choose, to "go home again." It was the place from which blacks took their self-chosen designation, from the earliest "African" to "Anglo-African" to "Colored" to "Negro" to "Afro-American" to "African American" and variations in between. All pointed back to "the Continent," the land from which all these names derived their meaning and their substance. By the mid- to late-20th century, there was increasing knowledge and consciousness that Africa was the source of much that unconsciously had been transmitted as black culture, including speech patterns, mannerisms, food preferences, hair styles, musical productions, social values, worship behaviors, and world view.

Through the years, Africa was looked on as one of two things. The first was as the ancestral home which its more fortunate descendants were bound by kinship and loyalty to help elevate—a type of cultural missionary idea. The other was as a homeland of great natural wealth and possibilities to which its separated children should return for their mutual care and development—a nationalistic idea. Supporters of both of these ideas are described below.

Edward Wilmot Blyden (1832–1912)

Edward Wilmot Blyden was born in St. Thomas, Virgin Islands, in 1832. His family attended the Dutch Reformed Church, but in his preteen years he became a student of a white Presbyterian missionary. In 1850, the missionary brought Blyden to the United States and tried to enroll him in Rutgers College, but he was refused there and at two other schools because of his color. This, plus seeing fugitive slaves seized and returned to bondage, made him resentful of the United States and he accepted an invitation from the American Colonization Society to go to Liberia to help develop that new nation. There he attended school, became a school principal, and also received ordination as a Presbyterian minister. He went on to become a scholar of international reputation. He held a number of government offices in West African countries, and traveled widely in Africa, Europe, and the United States.

Blyden was an Ethiopianist: he took seriously the biblical statement that "Ethiopia shall soon stretch out her hands unto God" (Psalms 68:10). Ethiopianists interpreted this to mean that Africa would one day emerge as a great world power. Blyden believed that God had intended for blacks to be brought to the United States to gain its technical knowledge, its skills, and its Christian faith. It was the black Americans' duty to take these valuables back to benefit Africa so that the Biblical prophecy might be fulfilled.

Blyden strongly defended African culture; it was at least the equal of any of the cultures of the world's great peoples, and it was well-suited to the needs of the African people. It was only Western technical know-how that would be of benefit to Africa in becoming a world leader.

To his disappointment, Blyden did not get much response to his plea that African Americans move back to Africa. He later modified his position to call for only a small cadre of blacks to go to the motherland to aid and energize the development process. Finally, Blyden gave up altogether on the goal of black American emigration to Africa. As he became settled in West Africa and active in its political and intellectual life, Ethiopianism came to mean for him the development of Africa by Africans. He died in 1912.

Creating a New Country

In the early 19th century, a group of white leaders created the American Colonization Society as a way to establish a place to which blacks from the United States could be relocated. These might be former slaves or free-born blacks, but in either case, blacks could not be American citizens. The ACS raised money to hire ships and find land. In 1821, the *Nautilus* arrived in Mesurado Bay on an island they named Perseverance on the east coast of Africa. The island and mainland there eventually became home to several thousand black emigrants from America. Though the early years were difficult, the settlers stayed and the colony grew. In 1847, they declared themselves the independent republic of Liberia, still a nation today.

Henry McNeal Turner (1834–1915)

Turner was an acquaintance of Edward Blyden, with whom he shared the dream of African-American emigration. Born in 1834 of free parents in Abbeville County, South Carolina, Turner acquired an education through private tutoring and his own effort—all contrary to the law, which did not allow education for blacks in those days.

Turner's religious vocation began in the Methodist Episcopal Church, South, but in 1858 he joined the AME church and became one of its most effective organizers. He was given credit for building the denomination's presence in Georgia from one congregation in 1865 to 187 by 1872, making it one of the strongest AME districts. In 1880 he was elected a bishop of the church.

Turner had been active in politics, organizing for the Republican Party (then the more socially liberal party in America), believing that bringing blacks into the political mainstream would be the best route to securing for them the protections of the law and the full benefits of citizenship. But his negative personal experiences in politics and the continuing record of the abusive treatment of black Americans eventually led to disillusionment with the country and all its structures. Seeing no prospects for change in the future, the path to a decent life for blacks seemed to Turner to lie in abandoning the American system for a place in which blacks could progress.

Africa, the land of blacks' origin, was rich and inviting. Its spacious territory would offer broad opportunities to black Americans, he believed, and the sympathetic preaching of the Christian faith by black American emigrants would benefit Africans. Turner compared black migration to Africa with the migration of the Pilgrims to North

America. In his view, both were cases of oppressed people seeking a land of freedom and opportunity.

Turner supported Pan Africanism, which seeks to unite blacks worldwide around their dignity and worth as black people and celebrates their African heritage. Turner even made the statement, bold for his day, that God was black. He was following the logic that the first humans were black Africans, which anthropological findings today support, and since the Bible says, "God created man in His own image," God must be black.

As a parish minister and as a bishop, Turner actively pursued his back-to-Africa vision for African Americans. He wrote about it regularly in the AME periodicals he founded and edited (the Southern *Christian Recorder* and the *Voice of Missions*) and in other publications. He visited the African continent to see the place of his dream firsthand. In 1878, he and Dr. Martin R. Delaney, another emigrationist, consecrated the ship *Azor*, which was to provide the transportation for the emigration.

Turner did not envision all African Americans returning to Africa, only a number sufficient to help establish a secure, efficient national homeland. Such a development would give blacks everywhere a standing amongst the peoples of the world, bringing them worldwide respect and respectful treatment. But many black Americans did not share Turner's dream. The numbers he hoped to recruit never came forth. His dream of African-American liberation through repatriation to Africa was not to be realized. He passed away in 1915.

Marcus Mosiah Garvey (1887–1940)

Probably the best-known person associated with the back-to-Africa idea was Marcus Garvey. In his native Jamaica, where he was born in 1887, he worked his way up to manager in a large printing firm while also learning and teaching public speaking skills. In his early 20s he left the printing business and pursued full time an interest in politics and the publication of a newspaper, *The Watchman*.

Garvey's observation of the depressed living conditions of blacks and indigenous people in Caribbean countries spurred his thinking about a model of black self-help and economic development. This resulted in the founding in 1914 of the Universal Negro Improvement Association (UNIA), which was intended to unite blacks across the

Man on a mission
Marcus Garvey was the most prominent and well-known leader in the movement to encourage African Americans to move back to Africa.

world around principles of positive self-image and economic cooperation. Garvey was influenced in his thinking by reading *Up from Slavery*, the autobiography of African-American Booker T. Washington (1856–1915), who promoted self-help and industrial education for blacks.

Coming to the United States from Jamaica in 1916, Garvey expanded his UNIA organization. He was a spellbinding orator; he spoke at black churches across the United States. The difficult economic and social circumstances of blacks made his audiences ready to hear him. In time, hundreds of UNIA chapters were started. By 1921, Garvey claimed to have 4 million followers. Even his critics said he had a half million followers, which put the success of his efforts higher than any who had come before him. His was the largest mass movement that had ever arisen among African Americans.

Garvey's appeal was to race pride. He spoke of blackness as a symbol of strength and beauty, rather than inferiority, and of Africa as a place with a noble past. Since racial prejudice appeared to be permanent in white people, the solution for blacks was to return to Africa to make it a place that would command fear and respect among the nations. There could be a black Congress, a black military, and a Black House (the proper alternative to the White House). He organized many support groups, such as the Universal Black Cross Nurses. The UNIA purchased the large Liberty Auditorium in Harlem as its headquarters. The organization operated many businesses. Possibly his most impressive venture was the Black Star Steamship Line, a wholly black-owned and managed commercial shipping company.

Garvey had always held a high regard for religion and saw it as crucial to his black social development program. In John Hope Franklin's 1966 book *From Slavery to Freedom,* Garvey is quoted as saying about a black God, "The God of Africa [who would] speak with a voice of thunder that shall shake the pillars of an unjust world, and once more restore Ethiopia to her ancient glory." Jesus and the angels were also said to be black. While he rejected the idea of a separate church, he did develop a hymnal, a creed, and a ritual for baptism.

Garvey's hope was that all this would lead to what many referred to as "the liberation of Africa" for black rule. He even set up what he called the Republic of Africa, a kind of government from a distance,

Garvey the Poet

Along with his speeches and essays, Marcus Garvey wrote poetry and songs. Here is an excerpt from "Africa for Africans," a poem from *Poetic Meditations of Marcus Garvey* (1927).

Say! Africa for the Africans,
Like America for the Americans:
This the rallying cry for a nation,
Be it in peace or revolution.

Blacks are men, no longer cringing fools;
They demand a place, not like weak tools;
But among the world of nations great
They demand a free self-governing state.

Hurrah! Hurrah! Great Africa wakes;
She is calling her sons, and none forsakes,
But to colors of the nation runs,
Even though assailed by enemy guns.

Cry it loud, and shout it lon' hurrah!
Time has changed, so hail! New Africa!
We are now awakened, rights to see:
We shall fight for dearest liberty.

with himself as the interim president. At one point he arranged with the Liberian government for a settlement to be established there.

Garvey's hopes and plans for the elevation of black people around the world from a base in Africa were ambitious and energetically pursued. Many black leaders in the United States believed that the concept was unrealistic and far-fetched. But large numbers of blacks signed on to his organization, and many influential black clergy supported him.

The plans were never realized. Financial reversals drained the UNIA of its funds and legal charges regarding his fundraising methods landed Garvey in prison, from which President Calvin Coolidge later pardoned him. But with the pardon came deportation. Garvey continued the pursuit of the aims for UNIA from Jamaica and later from London. But the organization was not able to regain its membership and influence.

Whatever the numbers of paying members UNIA had, its moral support was far wider. Garvey, and those before and since who have promoted bold programs challenging the oppressive treatment of African Americans and their exclusion from the benefits of American society, have always been powerful, attractive symbols and sources of motivation to work for positive social change.

FATHER DIVINE PEACE MOVEMENT

Born George Baker (1882–1965) in Georgia, the man who came to be called Father Divine was a powerful preacher and civil rights leader. During the Depression years, the Father Divine Peace Movement, as he called his organization, built a large organization of missions and homes. Drawing influence both from his preaching and his many successful business dealings, Father Divine had thousands of followers. However, his work also drew criticism from some who labeled it a cult, because Father Divine sometimes called himself the second coming of Christ. He died in 1965 and his movement shrank, but some of the missions still survive today.

Arenia Conelia Mallory (1905–1977)

Though born in Jacksonville, Illinois, in 1905, Arenia Mallory was to leave her mark on life in the deep South. She was the daughter of a show-business family and her parents groomed her to be a concert pianist. They had visions of her traveling the world, playing the great recital halls. And well she might have, had she not stopped, one high school night, to visit a religious tent meeting being held in her town. Mallory was so captivated by what she observed that she came back the next night, against the wishes of her parents. What took place that second night was an emotional experience of religious conversion that changed the course of her life.

Following high school graduation, Mallory accepted the invitation of some missionaries of the Church of God in Christ (COGIC) to live and work with them. She served as their musician and song leader on their cross-country revival tours. Then in 1926, the founder of the COGIC denomination, Bishop Charles H. Mason (1866–1961), invited her to come to Lexington, Mississippi, to be a music teacher at the church's school, the Saints Industrial and Literary School. Mallory's ambition had been to go to Africa as a missionary to her people; going to Mississippi seemed to be a detour. But she was told that in Lexington she would have the chance to be a missionary and fulfill her goals for her people. She was soon to see what that meant.

When she arrived in Lexington and was taken to the Saints Industrial campus , what she saw was not very encouraging: one rough-hewn building, crude facilities, very little equipment, and scarce supplies of food. It became clear how she could be a missionary to her people in that place.

In facing the great needs of the school, Mallory took to heart two passages of scripture: Matthew 9:37-38 and Philippians 4:13. The first passage speaks of God sending laborers for the harvest; the second assures that all things are achievable with Christ as one's source of strength. So she accepted the challenge before her, even becoming eager to take it on.

The challenge was soon larger still: During Mallory's first year at Saints Industrial, the school's chief administrator died and Mallory was tapped to take his place at the head of the school. With determination, she set out to make the school a first-rate place of learning. She recruited quality teachers, black and white; electric lights and central heating were installed; concrete roads and sidewalks replaced mud pathways; students planted on land around the school to grow their own food; and many other improvements were made.

Of course, all this did not happen at once. These things required a great deal of money, which was always in very short supply. One of the main ways Mallory chose to raise funds was the singing tour. She often told the story of how these tours worked. A few students would be gathered to form a chorus. Mallory would kneel for prayer at her bedside, putting the schools bills on the bed and asking God for help and for which direction they should travel. When she felt an answer, they set out on the journey. Arriving in the big cities, Mallory would arrange for the group to put on concerts in the large churches for audience donations. These singing tours were a major source of the monies Mallory used to build up Saints Industrial.

Under Mallory's leadership, the school steadily progressed. It was the first accredited high school for blacks in Holmes County, had

A SPIRITUAL LEADER

Bishop Charles Mason was a young minister in Los Angeles in 1906 when he attended the Azusa Street Revival. He was so moved, and indeed was baptized at one of those events, that he traveled back to his home in the South to start a new movement, based on the power of the Holy Spirit.

In 1906, he established the Church of God in Christ, and since then, the denomination has become one of the largest black Pentecostal groups in the United States with headquarters in Norfolk, Virginia.

Like other Pentecostals, they believe that the Bible is all literally true, the word of God. Their services are very enthusiastic, filled with singing, clapping, and lots of vocalizing from both the pulpit and the pews.

Mason died in 1961, and today the group's full official name is the Mason Memorial Church of God in Christ.

the first school band in the county, and was first in providing school bus transportation for blacks. By 1954, the school had achieved a high enough academic standing and became Saints Junior College.

Saints was a beacon of hope for many. It drew students from many parts of the nation, even achieving an integrated student body in the 1960s. By the time Mallory retired in 1976, some 20,000 students had passed through the instructional programs of Saints Industrial/Saints Junior College.

Nor was Mallory's leadership confined to the Saints campus. On the local scene she was a practicing midwife. In the broader world, she was the first black person in Mississippi elected to a county board of education; vice-president of the National Society for the Prevention of Juvenile Delinquency; a charter member of the National Council of Negro Women, which she served as vice president and also regional director, to name just some of her accomplishments. Today, a street in Lexington, Mississippi, bears her name. She died in 1977.

ANY WAY THEY COULD

Here is Arenia Mallory's description of one of the singing tours her students took to raise money for the school:

We would purchase oil and gas and everything on credit and then head for California, New York, or just about anywhere. We would leave for New York with only $1.50 . . . . for I had faith and believed that's where God wanted me to go. To go to New York would take us maybe two months because we'd stop along the way and go into little churches and ask them to give us a chance to speak to the people [to seek donations]. We stopped in the cotton fields and sang for the people picking cotton. They gave us their nickels and dimes.

Martin Luther King, Jr. (1929–1968)

The Rev. Dr. Martin Luther King, Jr., came from a line of distinguished ministers. Born January 15, 1929, his parents gave him the name Michael Lewis King, Jr. But at age five, his father changed both his and his son's names to Martin Luther, in honor of the renowned figure of the Protestant Reformation who modeled boldness in the fight for truth.

King grew up in Atlanta, and after high school, he attended Morehouse College in that city. The example of the Rev. Dr. Benjamin Mays (1894–1984), a noted minister and scholar and president of Morehouse, influenced King's decision to go into the ministry. After Morehouse, King attended Crozier Theological Seminary, and later received his doctor of philosophy degree from the Boston University School of Theology. There he met and married Coretta Scott, with whom he would have four children.

Following graduation, King accepted the call to be pastor of the Dexter Avenue Baptist Church in Montgomery, Alabama. That was a fateful decision, for it placed him in a position to step into a rising tide of historical developments. Blacks in that city, as in many cities of the South and North, were subject to severe racial segregation in public services and accommodations, and community leaders in Montgomery were discussing strategies for challenging those practices.

Shortly after Martin and Coretta arrived in Montgomery in 1955, a seamstress named Rosa Parks (b.1913), taking the bus on her way home from work, declined to honor a particular segregation law that required her to give up her seat to a white passenger. Following her arrest, local black leadership resolved to stage a boycott of the public transportation system until such discriminatory practices were ended. King was elected president of the boycott organization, the Montgomery Improvement Association. Within a year, the boycott reached a successful conclusion. The loss of income to the bus company caused it to relent and change its policies, and the U.S. Supreme Court ruled such policies illegal.

King was elected president of the new Southern Christian Leadership Conference (SCLC), whose purpose was to extend across the South the kind of civil rights activism of the Montgomery Improvement Association. In this role, King came to be identified with marches, demonstrations, and rallies aimed at changing laws and social practices that institutionalized racial discrimination. These methods suited him because during his years at Crozier Seminary he had read of the work of Mahatma Gandhi (1869–1948), who led the successful struggle of the people of India for independence from British rule. Gandhi operated by the Hindu principle of Satyagraha, the use of non-violent persuasion as opposed to physical confrontation. King had also encountered the writings of the 19th-century American author Henry David Thoreau (1817–1862), who argued for civil disobedience as the means to change unjust laws.

The methods advanced by Thoreau and Gandhi seemed to King to be the appropriate social application of his understanding of Christian social relations. They were how King thought his faith told him that people should pursue what he called "the Beloved Community," the ideal of human social life under God. Martin and Coretta King even traveled to India in 1959 to study Satyagraha so that they could effectively put it into practice in the U.S. civil rights struggle.

King became co-pastor, with his father, M.L. King, Sr., of the Ebenezer Baptist Church in Atlanta, headquarters of the SCLC. King was able to spend even more time on the organization's programs and goals. The peaceful boycott in Montgomery had proven successful. A 1957 march and rally in Washington, D.C., seemed to contribute in large measure to the creation of the Civil Rights Commission and the Civil

Honored by the world
In 1964, in honor of his ongoing struggle for civil rights using nonviolent methods, King was awarded the Nobel Peace Prize. Here he is giving a speech after accepting the important award at a ceremony in Sweden.

Rights Division of the Justice Department. King used the moving oratorical skills of the black preaching tradition to become an eloquent, international spokesperson for the non-violent approach to social change.

It was the commitment of King and other black Baptist clergy to seeking change through peaceful confrontation of unjust systems that led to a major realignment in the Baptist family. King, partnered with Rev. Gardner Taylor of Brooklyn's Concord Baptist Church, pressed the National Baptist Convention, USA, Inc., to endorse this activist civil rights strategy. But the more socially conservative president of the Convention, Rev. Joseph H. Jackson (1900–1990), was unalterably in opposition, even though he had a genuine concern for black rights. Consequently, in 1961 King, Taylor, and other members of the Convention withdrew to form the Progressive National Baptist Convention.

King's commitment to the nonviolent civil rights struggle further expressed itself in such notable events as the campaign in Birmingham, Alabama, with its scenes of demonstrators assaulted by fire hoses and attack dogs, captured so vividly in the video series "Eyes on the Prize." This video, incidentally, showed the large degree to which the Civil Rights movement depended on school-age children in its protest demonstrations. There was also the historic march on Washington of 1963, drawing nearly 300,000 participants and culminating in King's now classic "I Have a Dream" speech. The Selma, Alabama, to Montgomery march of 1965 again drew national attention and helped lead to the passage that year of the Voting Rights Act.

Although a Southerner, King's vision was much broader. In 1966 he brought the movement to Chicago. He and his family took up residence in a West Side tenement building, an important symbol that he was in solidarity with those he sought to aid. But the North did not seem to be as agreeable to the SCLC style of protest, and so King's stay in Chicago was brief.

In another area, King's ministry met with opposition from within his own ranks. By the late 1960s, the United States had become deeply embroiled in the Vietnam War. King, as did many other citizens, raised questions about U.S. involvement in this conflict. In fact, King criticized it on several grounds. He saw it as an unjust use of power on a weaker nation for selfish purposes. But even if the purposes had been noble, King's life was dedicated to pursuing peace as both a means of resolving conflict and as an aim itself. He saw that he could never again speak out for nonviolent solutions to American racial issues if he supported violent solutions to international issues. Further, he felt that the same forces responsible for social and economic injustices in America were merely extending themselves into the international arena. In this view, every dollar spent for bombs in a morally unsupportable war overseas was money not available to support programs to address the pressing needs at home.

Many people within SCLC and the larger civil rights movement objected to King's increasingly outspoken stance on Vietnam. Some believed that this was "off the subject" and would take away from the force of the movement. Others argued that he was a leader only for racial issues and that he should not be meddling in other matters. But King would not be deterred. He had come to see that issues of race, poverty, social oppression, international relations, global economics, and war were all intertwined and part of the larger issue of justice. One could not be addressed to the exclusion of the others.

King's work, however controversial, continued to draw more and more attention, both in the United States and around the world. In recognition of his efforts in the Civil Rights movement and for justice everywhere, he was honored with the Nobel Peace Prize in 1964.

King's life was a relatively brief 39 years. He was killed by an assassin's bullet on April 4, 1968, as he prepared to participate in a campaign in Memphis, Tennessee, on behalf of better working conditions for the city's sanitation workers. But the nation and the world have honored him for the quality of his life and work. In November, 1983, President Ronald Reagan signed into law an act making King's birthday, January 15, a national holiday celebrated on the third Monday in January.

I HAVE A DREAM

Here is a short excerpt from the speech given by Martin Luther King, Jr., on the steps of the Lincoln Memorial on August 28, 1963.

I have a dream that one day the state of Alabama, whose governor's lips are presently dripping with the words of interposition and nullification, will be transformed into a situation where little black boys and black girls will be able to join hands with little white boys and white girls and walk together as sisters and brothers. I have a dream today. I have a dream that one day every valley shall be exalted, every hill and mountain shall be made low, the rough places will be made plain, and the crooked places will be made straight, and the glory of the Lord shall be revealed, and all flesh shall see it together.

Warith Deen Muhammad (b.1930) and Louis Farrakhan (b.1933)

In 1975, following the death of Nation of Islam leader Elijah Muhammad (see page 42), it was assumed that Elijah's son, Wallace D. Muhammad, would take over. It was thought that he had been chosen from birth to assume the honored position at the helm of the Nation.

Wallace had been named after Wallace D. Fard, founder of the Nation of Islam. Although he was thought to be the eventual leader, there were few signs that he would ready to take on this important role. He was educated in the Nation's school in Chicago, the Muhammad University of Islam, and he held various secondary positions within the organization, including that of minister of the Philadelphia Temple. But Wallace differed with his father on the degree to which some of the Nation's policies and practices were in keeping with his understanding of Islam. He even broke away from the Nation for a time.

By the time of Elijah Muhammad's death, he and Wallace had reconciled and Wallace was back in the fold. Elijah put into place his long-standing intention that Wallace would assume his mantle upon his death. On Savior's Day, 1975, a major Nation of Islam event, this rather soft-spoken son with the low-key demeanor took the reins of the dynamic Nation of Islam.

Wallace Muhammad soon introduced new administrative procedures. More startlingly, he began a process that reflected the direction that his thought had been taking since high school—that the

Nation should align itself, in structure and practice, with worldwide Islam, particularly the Sunni branch. Over the next 10 years he made such major changes as opening the membership of the Nation of Islam to whites; reinterpreting the role and authority of his father Elijah and of Fard in the Nation's theology; and instituting Muslim names for the organization's structures, including a change of the name of the organization, itself, to the American Muslim Mission. Standard Muslim rituals were introduced into the Nation of Islam's services.

In various stages Wallace, who changed his own name to Warith, disbanded the national structure of the organization and transferred his power first to a council of imams (religious heads of mosques) then to all imams individually, as heads of their local mosques, in keeping with general Muslim practice.

Why did Warith Muhammad change the group so radically? His explanation is that the mode of Islam his father had established was meant for a particular time and set of circumstances in the life of the African-American community. It was never meant to be permanent.

Leading black Muslim *Imam W. D. Muhammad leads the American Muslim Mission, the largest single Islamic group in the United States. He split with earlier teachings of the Nation of Islam in 1975, when he succeeded his father, Elija h Muhammad, as leader of the organization.*

He asserts that his father always intended that his followers would ultimately practice the Islamic religion in the manner of other Muslims around the world. Thus, Muhammad believes that he was not departing from his father's vision but rather fulfilling it.

There were others within the Nation, however, who saw it differently. The most prominent group to dissent emerged under the leadership of Louis Farrakhan. He was born Louis Walcott of Jamaican parents in New York City in 1933 and raised in the Boston area. He was a promising student and a gifted musician who played the violin. He left college to try his fortunes in the entertainment world, but gave up show business after hearing the Nation of Islam's message and becoming involved in the organization.

Recognizing Louis' gifts, Elijah Muhammad appointed him to larger positions of responsibility. It was Muhammad who also changed Louis' last name from the " X" he had adopted to Farrakhan. Muhammad certainly also recognized Farrakhan's oratorical prowess. He was a stirring public speaker who could enthrall Muslim and non-Muslim audiences for hours with his caustic application of the Nation's religious teachings and social analysis of U.S. racial practices.

Farrakhan became displeased with the direction in which Warith Muhammad was moving the Nation as successor to his father, believing that the Nation was abandoning its basic identity and principles, as set forth by Elijah Muhammad. So in 1978 Farrakhan began a new group which reclaimed the name Nation of Islam that had been dropped by Warith Muhammad. This organization is headquartered in Chicago, where it still maintains the old Temple (Mosque) No. 2 and the University of Islam.

Farrakhan's Nation of Islam group focuses heavily on fostering black economic development and social empowerment. The Nation models these principles in its own projects, as, for instance, the elegant Salaam Restaurant it operates on Chicago's South Side. Farrakhan, himself, continues to hold a reputation as a public speaker, and is well-known for his involvement in organizing the 1995 Million Man March in Washington, D.C. (see page 83).

In 2000, Muhammad and Farrakhan had a very public meeting at which they said they were, in effect, resolving their differences and agreeing to work together.

Frederick Price (b.1932)

Many Christian preachers have taken to the television airwaves to spread the word and attract new followers. Most of those preachers, however, are white. Among the handful of African-American "televangelists" is Frederick K.C. Price of the Crenshaw Christian Center (CCC) in Los Angeles.

Price grew up in Los Angeles, but did not consider himself a "churchgoer." He met his future wife, Betty, at Dorsey High School, and to try to impress her and her family, he started going to church with them. At a tent revival meeting as a young man, he was "born again," and became active in ministry for a succession of churches and denominations.

According to Price's biography on the CCC's web site at www.increasethefaith.com, in 1970 he "received the gift of the Holy Spirit with the evidence of speaking in tongues." In 1973, he formed the CCC. In 1984, having expanded the congregation dramatically, he moved it to a former college campus in south-central Los Angeles, renaming the place The FaithDome. It seats more than 10,000 people and is one of the largest sanctuaries in the United States.

In 1990, he took to the television airwaves, broadcasting the *Ever Increasing Faith Ministries* show from his Los Angeles church. A dynamic, thoughtful, and impressive speaker, Price's broadcasts regularly attract good ratings and are watched by Christian audiences of all backgrounds. Price has used the power of broadcasting to expand his coverage, as well as inspiring other preachers to use radio, television, video, and audiotapes to help them spread the word.

FREEDOM RIDES

During the Civil Rights movement of the 1960s, groups of the movement's supporters would make long bus trips from the North to the South to join in protests against racial discrimination. These trips became known as Freedom Rides.

Prathia Hall (1940–2002)

Philadelphia native Prathia Hall was a top debater in high school, and she used her speaking skills in the fight for civil rights. At Temple University, Hall became a part of the emerging social justice movement. She joined with others to become a Northern support group for students in the South fighting racist laws.

In 1961, she took her first Freedom Ride to Annapolis, where the group was denied service at the bus station and arrested. They remained in jail for two weeks, in keeping with the "jail, no bail" strategy which the organizers had adopted. In 1962, Hall left Temple to go

South to work more closely with the Student Non-Violent Coordinating Committee (SNCC), a national group of college students.

Hall told the author about some of her experiences. "It was very dangerous. We lived with fear; we could taste it. There was good reason for the fear—the house [where we stayed] was shot into; three of us were hit. Three of the churches in southwest Georgia, where I went to work, were burned to the ground in one night. It was dangerous for people to receive us. But they would say, 'I'm afraid. But I want a different life for my children. And so, I'm gonna go down to the courthouse in the morning and sign my name, register to vote. I'm gonna trust God to take me there and I'm gonna trust God to bring me back.'

"That experience was a great gift to our lives. A lot of what I am today comes from being embraced by those people."

Hall points out that many women played key roles in the movement and in SNCC, including Ella Baker, a field secretary for the NAACP. "There would not have been a movement had it not been for the women, who had been carrying the work from the 1930s," Hall says. "Women like Baker often sneaked into towns at night and sometimes had to sneak out in undertakers' coffins to avoid detection."

Hall herself left college to seek justice. In Alabama and Georgia, she and her black and white co-workers "went house to house meeting people, listening to their stories, gaining their trust, building their courage and stamina to take action." They held literacy classes and meetings in churches.

Hall also used her considerable speaking abilities as a traveling spokesperson for the SNCC. She served with SNCC in the South from 1962 to 1965, then worked in their New York office into 1966. She later earned a masters degree and a doctorate and was ordained as a minister through the American Baptist Convention.

Until her death in 2002, Hall was respected as a teacher, lecturer, and author in her specialty fields of ethics, Womanist Theology, and African-American religious history. She was also minister at the Mt. Sharon Baptist Church in Philadelphia, the church she attended as a child. She also held the Martin Luther King, Jr., Chair in Social Ethics at the Boston University School of Theology.

Jesse Jackson

The son of an Alabama sharecropper, Jesse Jackson (b.1941) was born Jesse Burns in Greenville, South Carolina (he later adopted his stepfather's last name, Jackson). After high school, Jackson was offered a baseball contract by the Chicago White Sox, but he turned it down because a white player was given a higher salary. He also later turned down a football scholarship at the University of Illinois when he was told that a black man could not expect to play quarterback.

Jackson attended the University of Illinois anyway, but, dissatisfied with the way he was treated on campus, he soon transferred to the mostly black North Carolina Agricultural and Technical College, where he got a degree in sociology. While he was there, he took a lead in protests that forced Greensboro, North Carolina, to integrate its restaurants and theaters.

In March 1965, inspired by Rev. Martin Luther King, Jr.'s Cvil Rights march in Selma, Alabama, Jackson met King and asked him for a job with the Southern Christian Leadership Conference (SCLC). The following year, Jackson, who was then studying at Chicago Theological Seminary, was among the leaders of King's open housing marches in Chicago. He was also named head of the Chicago branch of Operation Breadbasket, an SCLC program that organized black consumers to press for jobs and to encourage and expand black-owned businesses. He became its national head in 1967.

Jackson was also ordained a Baptist minister in 1968. That same year, he was standing beside King when the great leader was assassinated.

After a falling-out with the SCLC resulted in his removal from Operation Breadbasket in 1971, Jackson founded his own organization, PUSH (People United to Save Humanity). Like Operation Breadbasket, the new organization set its sights on strengthening the economic security of African Americans.

Jackson became more active in politics, as well. In 1972, he led a group that successfully challenged Chicago Mayor Richard J. Daley's slate of delegates at the Democratic National Convention. And in 1984 and 1988, backed by yet another of his organizations, the Rainbow Coalition, he ran in the Democratic presidential primaries, gaining enough votes to make him a presence at the convention.

He also has been active in international issues, for instance successfully negotiating the release of an American soldier held prisoner in Syria in 1984, as well as soldiers captured in Iraq in 1990. He remains among the most vocal and well-known African-American political leaders.

7

African-American Faith Today and Tomorrow

IN THESE EARLY YEARS OF THE NEW MILLENNIUM, RELIGIOUS congregations are still important centers of energy and service in black communities. For millions of African Americans the congregation—Christian, Muslim, Jewish, or otherwise—is still the main place where people volunteer, contribute to charity, and find meaningful support for the difficulties of life.

As some predominantly white Christian denominations move toward racial and ethnic diversity in appointing clergy for local parishes, the African-American perspective on religious faith and practice is being shared with a larger community of believers. One can imagine a similar sharing at work in the Islamic community as African Americans come to hold a larger share of Muslim membership and leadership. This will enrich all who participate in the sharing.

Maintaining the Mission

African-American religion, in its many denominational and organizational forms, still pursues its traditional three-fold mission of evangelism, celebration, and liberation.

Evangelism. As discussed in the introduction, for the Christian churches where most blacks hold religious affiliation, and the various Muslim communities, evangelism is a primary focus of the groups' concern and activities. They seek to get the message out about their group's beliefs and programs and present a compelling case as to why people should commit their lives to their faith. To do this, each uses worship services and scheduled religious educational study. In addition, each group has regularly published news journals that present the ongoing life and service work of the institution, along with inspirational and devotional materials. Further, many churches use the Internet to offer information about their tenets, history, and structure.

In the closing decades of the 20th century, many established Christian denominations experienced a significant drop in membership, due to complex social and religious forces that they are still trying to comprehend. The African-American denominations were not an exception; most of them also lost membership. This led to an increased emphasis on church growth and evangelism, boosted especially by word of the development of huge congregations of new members in places such as Korea. Publishing houses began turning out a stream of books and journals on church growth and evangelism. African-American clergy were buying and reading them. Some decided to share their experiences in building up the size of their congregations and became authors on the subject themselves.

PRECEDING PAGE
Ready to serve
The long tradition of service by members of African-American congregations continues today. In this 1999 photo, members of Abyssinian Baptist Church in New York City are ordained as deacons and deaconesses.

The issue of membership loss continues. But at the same time, the nation is witnessing the rise of what are called "mega-churches." These are congregations of extraordinary size, with memberships of 7,000 to 10,000, some even ranging as high as 20,000 or more. There are several such African-American mega-churches, and their number is increasing. They can be found in all regions of the country. Congregations of this size call for re-thinking the meaning of "church family," a term that carries the idea of members having an intimate relationship with one another—something difficult to achieve when the numbers are this large. Mega-churches call for re-thinking how to do group-building; how to handle issues of communication of the church's message in large worship and instructional settings; and generally how to provide caring ministry and effective leadership to a mass constituency.

Furthermore, one of the historically black Christian denominations seems to have been unaffected by the cycle of membership loss. The Church of God in Christ (COGIC) experienced steady gains in its numbers, and by the end of the 20th century it claimed some 8 million members on its rolls, placing it among the largest of the black Christian bodies.

The evangelistic outreach of the African-American Christian bodies continues today in its historic mission to the world beyond the United States. They have vibrant and growing congregations and administrative divisions in the Caribbean, South America, Canada, Europe, and especially Africa.

Celebration. African-American worship celebrates peoples' living, loving relationship with God. It also is a means of giving honor and thanks to God for all the ways God's majesty and power are demonstrated in the workings of creation, and God's saving strength and mercy are demonstrated in their lives.

The style of black worship has always varied among denominations and congregations. Historically the more formally structured, emotionally low-key worship was associated with the Methodist groups, the more openly expressive and lively with the Baptist groups, with the COGIC churches and their Pentecostal Holy Spirit visitation and speaking in tongues being the most high-intensity moments.

But across the board, there has been ample spontaneity, intensity, and fervent expressiveness in most black religious groups, especially as compared to the style common in Euro-American groups. This has been true also of the black Muslim groups. While following their notable public discipline and decorum, typically charismatic leadership has generated considerable enthusiasm and fervor in worship behavior. This is somewhat less true for the significant numbers of blacks who today are affiliated with Sunni Islam, which maintains a more contemplative, ritual style of worship.

Nowadays, the style differences among the various black religious bodies has been diminished by the increase in two religious elements: gospel music and Neo-Pentecostalism. From the early days when most black churches rejected it as too worldly, gospel music has moved to a central place in black church music, regardless of denomination. In some churches it has replaced altogether the hymn and anthem choirs. Even when other genres of music are used, it is not uncommon for them to be "gospelized," that is, played and sung with the rhythms, syncopation, and mood of gospel. So, gospel music and

From Hoops to Hosannas

In the Los Angeles suburb of Inglewood, one church has taken advantage of the departure of the NBA's Los Angeles Lakers to create for itself a new worship space. The Lakers moved from the 16,000-seat Los Angeles Forum in 2000 to the new Staples Arena downtown. The Forum was virtually unused.

In 2000, the Faithful Central Bible Church, a predominantly African-American church in Los Angeles, bought the Forum and now holds Sunday services on the same floor where the Lakers once held court. More than 10,000 people come to these massive gatherings of prayer, music, sermon, and learning. The rest of the week, the church leases the arena for concerts and conventions, combining worship and economics in a new and creative way.

the worship tone it carries with it are bringing a greater level of common identity to the diverse African-American religious bodies.

Another factor is Neo-Pentecostalism, which began making its impact in the late decades of the 20th century. At one time, intense, focused "praise and worship," with music often composed specifically for this function, was common in Pentecostal churches. Baptist congregations commonly set aside a time before the start of the worship service, or as the opening portion of the service, a period of "devotions." This involved prayers and scriptures, usually led by

Singing praises
Gospel singers, such as these performing in Virginia, remain a key part of the services of many different African-American Christian denominations.

church officers (the deacons), and spontaneous songs raised from the congregation.

As blacks moved through the 20th century, especially as they moved from the rural South into the cities of the South and North, the periods of devotions declined in use, eventually being eliminated from many congregations. But the Neo-Pentecostal upsurge in black congregations of all denominations has introduced to some, and re-introduced to others, the practice of a devotional period for song and prayer as a primer for worship. This has come along with other elements of worship tone and worship behaviors (such as verbal "Hallelujahs" and praise applause), again blurring to a degree the worship differences among the various black denominations.

One very important offshoot of this matter of celebration and the fact that differences still exist, despite the growing similarity, is the emergence of the Full Gospel Baptist Church Fellowship. Officially founded in 1994 under the leadership of the Rev. Paul S. Morton, Sr., it is a membership organization drawing congregations from across denominational lines that heralds gospel music and seeks the freedom to use worship styles and practices not part of a congregation's denominational tradition. These include, particularly, the more expressive, emotional Pentecostal worship style and the Pentecostal speaking in tongues and laying on of hands (touching churchgoers to give a blessing; sometimes believed to have healing powers).

Essentially drawing from Baptist churches, the Full Gospel group diverges radically from Baptist organizational principles in that the Fellowship administration is placed in the hands of officers with titles such as bishop and elder. All this has led, consequently, to controversy in Baptist ranks over whether pastors and congregations that affiliate with the Fellowship can retain their membership in their respective Baptist Conventions or should be required to withdraw from one or the other. Complicating the issue is the fact that the Full Gospel Baptist Church Fellowship is not identified by itself or by others as a denomination, even though it has a formal organizational structure, membership procedures, a mission and purpose statement, an annual conference of member churches, and claims 1 million members in more than 5,000 congregations.

However this denominational dispute is resolved, it is representative of the importance that African-American religious groups place on worship as a setting for celebrating the relationship between the divine and the human.

Liberation. The third component of the general mission of African-American religion is the liberation of the powers and capacities of African-Americans to be whole men and women, with equal access to the prerogatives, privileges, and opportunities that belong to all citizens. This component, like the others, is rooted in the theological vision that God is the universal parent who has, through direct intervention in history and through a procession of prophets and messianic figures, revealed the divine will that freedom and abundance in life are the heritage of all persons. Therefore, African-American religious institutions have seen the freedom struggle, in a variety of ways, as their cooperation with the divine will, rather than simply a self-interested desire for achievement on earthly terms.

In previous chapters we have seen how religiously motivated individuals and institutions have worked through cultural, social, and political processes to positively change society and bring about freedom with justice. The record continues today.

For instance, at the Nation of Islam's 2002 Savior's Day celebration, Minister Louis Farrakhan impressed upon the audience that they were collective instruments chosen by God to correct the inequities in the U.S. social and political system and usher black people into positions of respect and significance in society.

The Church of God in Christ sponsors a Home Buyers Program, which provides education and guidance in the steps toward home ownership, including counseling from mortgage and realty professionals. At its annual convention, the denomination sponsors a Youth Scholastic Motivation Ministry and workshops for the adult laity such as grant writing; business start-up, finance, and management; computer technology for churches; and management of not-for-profit corporations.

Among the programs of the AME Church is the Service and Development Agency (SADA), which operates in Haiti and focuses on health care and human services.

The CME Church has its Community Development Corporation, which partners with Fannie Mae to assist community members to achieve home ownership.

BIBLE STUDY ON THE INTERNET

The Full Gospel Baptist Church is among several groups that have created online Bible colleges and schools. Through www.fullgospel.net, students around the world can log on, read, and learn about the Bible and theology. Courses offered include some on New Testament Greek, giving sermons and homilies, history of prayer and worship, and history of black preaching. Students can even earn a doctorate of theology through the Full Gospel program.

Snacks after service
Following a prayer service at a mosque in Atlanta, worshipers stop and buy fruit and other goods from stands set up outside. A growing number of African Americans practice a wide variety of styles of Islam.

These programs. and many more that are sponsored by denominational offices, individual congregations, and ecumenical organizations such as the Congress of National Black Churches, represent the ongoing concern of African-American religion for the personal and social freedom of black people.

The Growing Presence of Islam

It is not just Christian churches that are growing among African Americans. There are perhaps 1.5 million African-American Muslims in the United States today, though exact numbers are hard to pin down. Today more than one-quarter of all mosques in the United States are primarily African-American.

In recent years, the split between the two major American Muslim groups has been eased. Warith Deen Muhammad, leader of the American Muslim Mission, and Louis Farrakhan, leader of the Nation of Islam, met in 2000 and formally ended their dispute (see page 106). Their reconciliation has helped America's black Muslim communities to begin a possible move toward more cooperation.

The Challenges of the Present and Future

African-American religion, in its various institutions and belief systems, offers noble visions of the way life can and ought to be, visions based on the revelations of a divine being who is beyond the world yet always intimately present to it and often critical of how the world operates.

Today those visions, perhaps more than ever before, are in competition with other claims for people's allegiance, other sets of values and models of how society might be. Those alternative values and visions are intensified by the exciting and persuasive media portrayals of the fast-lane life, the self-indulgent life, the life centered on self-determined values, and by a mood of the times which supports a critical rethinking of the concepts of religion and the divine.

African-American religion, as other faith communities, is challenged to provide a leadership vision for the 21st century. In a fast-changing and increasingly globalized world, religious groups need to be assisted in understanding what faith means and how the faithful one is called to action.

There are many concerns specific to African-Americans that religious communities can take up, especially given the importance of faith institutions, whether Christian or Muslim. Some of the issues facing all these groups include:

- The dilemma of HIV/AIDS that is ravaging black communities, in the United States and abroad.
- What veteran civil rights activist Angela Davis (b.1944) calls the "prison/industrial complex," the alliance between economic interests and the criminal justice system that is alleged to disproportionately arrest and convict African-Americans, keeping incompetent lawyers at work and feeding for-profit penal corporations.
- The continuing performance gap in academic achievement between African Americans and other Americans.
- The struggle to ensure that African Americans benefit equally from economic and technological advances in the United States.

None of these issues will be faced nor overcome without effort. They require preparation; an ability to dream; a determination to translate those dreams into positive reality; and not least, an active, living faith.

A Look Ahead

The opening lines of the second verse of James Weldon Johnson's "Negro National Anthem (Lift Ev'ry Voice and Sing)" describe what has been the setting and circumstance for much of the experience of Africans in the United States:

Stony the road we trod,
Bitter the chastening rod,
Felt in the days when hope unborn had died . . . .

The accomplishments and contributions of African Americans to the nation and the world constitute an amazing story. But when viewed against their historical setting they are extraordinary. And the historically black religious institutions of the country, Christian, Muslim, and otherwise, have been among the chief encouragers and sustainers of these contributions. They have inspired the efforts and led black people in finding the meaning of their existence and validating their place in the divine order of things.

Many of the blatant physical and social abuses of the past have moderated. And many African Americans have, through faith, grit, and struggle, "come to the place for which our [forbears] sighed," as the anthem continues.

The journey, though, has not ended. African Americans have shown their determination to, in the words of an old spiritual, "run on to see what the end will be." Led by faith, African-American religion, through its proclamations and its institutions, is certain to continue its effort to be the light and life along the way.

GLOSSARY

abolition The complete end of something, usually used to refer to the end of slavery

affirmative action Set of American laws and rules designed to balance past discrimination against African Americans.

baptism Christian rite of initiation for children and adults in which water is poured over a person or the person is immersed in a pool of water.

Black Theology System of thought developed in the 1970s that for the first time merged religious beliefs of African Americans with their struggle against discrimination and racism.

bondage The state of being captured or enslaved.

camp meeting Gatherings often held in large tents or in fields at which evangelists spoke about Christian themes.

caste Word for organized and regimented social classes.

charismatic Very demonstrative, enthusiastic, attractive; often used to describe certain forms of Christian preaching or worship.

congregation A group of people gathered together in a common church, usually on a local level.

cult Word used to describe a religious or quasi-religious organization that demands total devotion from its followers.

deacons Christian church officers below the rank of priests or ministers.

denomination An individual Christian group defined by its own creed or set of beliefs and practices.

diaspora Term used to describe the forced scattering or mass migration of a people or nation.

emancipation The process of gaining freedom.

Ethiopianist People who took seriously the biblical statement that "Ethiopia shall soon stretch out her hands unto God." (Psalms 68:10). Ethiopianists interpreted this to mean that Africa would one day emerge as a great world power.

eucharist A Christian ceremony or ritual that recreates the Last Supper, at which Jesus shared bread and wine with his apostles for the last time. Christians recreate this event to remember the promises Jesus made. Different denominations have different ways of celebrating or understanding this ceremony.

evangelism The process of trying to recruit new members of a faith.

full immersion baptism A baptism in which the person is completely covered by water, often by dunking in a small pool or tub.

glossolalia Word for "speaking in tongues," a phenomenon experienced by some that is said to come from experiencing the Holy Spirit.

gospel music Songs and singing style that first became popular in the 1930s. The style combines rhythms of jazz and other music with spiritual themes and lyrics.

heathen A person who does not believe in the God of the Bible.

Holiness The Protestant Christian belief that a person can be made specially holy by the Holy Spirit; a segment of Protestant denominations are known by this term.

Holy Spirit Christians believe that this is an aspect of the divine that can have a powerful, personal effect on people.

imam Title for minister a or religious leader in Islam.

indigenous Living originally in an area.

kindred Relatives or those affiliated with a family or community.

Kiswahili Language spoken in East Africa; sometimes called Swahili.

laity Non-clergy members of a church.

lobbied Actively worked to convince someone of something; often used to describe the act of trying to convince legislators to support a particular cause.

lynching Act of mob violence in which a person is forcibly taken and hanged.

Maafa Maafa means "disaster" in Kiswahili. It has been adopted by some scholars to describe the scope and tragedy of the North American slave trade.

mega-churches Churches with many thousands of people at regular services, often held in large auditoriums or arenas.

midwife A trained person who assists a mother in childbirth.

migration The mass movement of people (or animals) from one place to another.

mosque Islamic house of worship.

Pan Africanism Political theory developed in the early 20th century that helped inspire African Americans to move back to Africa.

Pentecostalism A form of Protestant Christianity that focuses on receiving and believing in the power of the Holy Spirit. Pentecost was the event in the Bible at which Jesus' apostles received the Holy Spirit in the form of "tongues of flame."

prophetic Predicting the future, usually accurately.

Reconstruction The period after the Civil War in which the South was rebuilt and reorganized after the destruction of war.

repertoire The list of works regularly performed by an artist, such as a dancer or musician.

Qur'an The holy book of Islam, sometimes spelled Koran.

sermon A speech made during a worship service.

sojourner A temporary resident.

suffrage The granting of the right to vote to a class of people; normally used to describe giving women the right to vote.

tenant farming Method of farming in which the farmers rent land from an owner and pay a portion of their crops as rent.

unalienable Not able to be taken away.

Time Line

1619	A Dutch ship arrives at Jamestown, Virginia, trading 20 Africans for food; it marks the introduction of slavery into what became the United States.
1787	Black worshippers at the St. George Methodist Episcopal Church, Philadelphia, walk out as a result of racially discriminatory treatment.
1794	The Saint Thomas Protestant Episcopal Church is founded in Philadelphia.
1816	Bethel Church, Philadelphia, joins with other black Methodists to form the independent African Methodist Episcopal Church.
1821	The African Methodist Episcopal Zion Church is organized.
1831	Nat Turner, an enslaved Baptist preacher, leads one of the most extensive slave revolts, causing the virtual shutdown of missions to the South.
1863	Emancipation and the conclusion of the Civil War (in 1865) open up the South to mission work by black denominations, which mushroom in size.
1870	The Colored (later Christian) Methodist Episcopal Church is formed.
1875	James Augustine Healy is made the first African-American Catholic bishop.
1895	The National Baptist Convention, USA, Inc., eventually to become the largest black denomination, is formed by the merger of three groups.
1897	The Church of God in Christ is incorporated.
1900	Migration of African Americans from the rural South begins to pick up. From 1900 to 1930, some 2 million blacks make the move to north and west.
1906	William Seymour leads the Azuza Street Revival, out of which developed the Pentecostal movement.
1930	Wallace D. Fard Muhammad begins the preaching in Detroit that launches the Nation of Islam.
1963	Baptist minister Martin Luther King, Jr., leads a march on Washington, where he delivers his celebrated "I Have a Dream" speech.
1964	Malcolm X breaks with the Nation of Islam and forms the Muslim Mosque, Inc., and the Organization of Afro-American Unity
1978	Warith Deen Muhammad, son of Elijah Muhammad, moves the Nation of Islam into the larger family of worldwide orthodox Islam, changing his organization's name finally to the Muslim American Society.
2000	Rev. Vashti Murphy McKenzie elected bishop in the African Methodist Episcopal Church, the first woman bishop in an historically black denomination.

RESOURCES

Reading List

King, Martin Luther, Jr., *Strength to Love*. New York: Harper and Row, 1963.

McKenzie, Vashti Murphy, *Not Without a Struggle*. Cleveland: United Church Press, 1996.

Murphy, Larry G., ed., *Down by the Riverside: Readings in African American Religions*. New York: New York University Press, 2000.

———, J. Gordon Melton, and Gary L. Ward, eds., *Encyclopedia of African-American Religion*. New York: Garland Publishing, 1993.

Pinn, Anne H., and Anthony B. Pinn, *Fortress Introduction to Black Church History*. New York: Fortress Press, 2001.

Raboteau, Albert J., *Canaan Land: A Religious History of African Americans*. New York: Oxford University Press, 1999.

Resources on the Web

Religious Organization Sites
Most of the major African-American churches have their own Web sites that provide background on the church and links to local organizations around the country. Here is a list of a few:

The African Methodist Episcopal Church
www.ame-church.org

The African Methodist Episcopal Zion Church
www.theamezionchurch.org

The Christian Methodist Episcopal Church
www.cmesonline.org

The Church of God in Christ
www.cogic.com

The Nation of Islam
www.finalcall.com

These sites provide general history of African-American religious life.

Black and Christian
www.blackandchristian.com

Black History (Encyclopedia Britannica)
www.blackhistory.eb.com

PBS: Africa
www.pbs.org/wnet/africa/

INDEX

Note: *Italic* page numbers refer to illustrations.